T0043917

"I absolutely love this book. Micha i deepest places of courage, beauty, pa page is a devastating and merciful invitation to transforming love, the kind that changes not only the world but also our own selves. It cleared a path for me to love an inefficient, complicated, beloved life and to want to follow Jesus all over again. A gift, a gift."

—**Sarah Bessey**, editor of the *New York Times* bestseller *A Rhythm of Prayer* and author of *Jesus Feminist*

"In this achingly beautiful book, Micha Boyett offers soulful, searching reflections on the life of faith in an unjust world. The result is a courageous exploration of spirituality, disability, community, friendship, the good life, and much more. *Blessed Are the Rest of Us* will move readers to tears, laughter, and back again, cutting a path through it all to the wisdom of Jesus, the dream of God, and strength to live in a troubled world."

—**Peter Choi**, executive director, Center for Faith and Justice; author of *George Whitefield: Evangelist for God and Empire*

"A soul-stirring story of faith and connection. I found great comfort in hearing from Micha, whose child's journey paralleled, yet differed from, my own child's. She expertly weaves God's word into her candid stories. Her unwavering love for God shines through every page, allowing her to extend grace and understanding to those who may see the world differently. So inspiring and uplifting. A must-read for those seeking solace and spiritual wisdom."

—**Kelli Caughman**, cofounder, Black Down Syndrome Association

"*Blessed Are the Rest of Us* is an important book. With earnest intention for justice and change, Micha Boyett offers a warm and honest reflection about being a mom to a child living with disability. But don't mistake this for just another parenting memoir.

This is a powerful narrative, one that will cause you to rethink so much of what you believe about disabilities, equality, and the dignity of others."

—**Matthew Paul Turner**, #1 *New York Times* bestselling author
of *What Is God Like?*

"Micha Boyett's *Blessed Are the Rest of Us* is a deeply moving meditation on being a part of, and participating in, the dream of God for us. It makes perfect sense that a poet like Micha would lead us to engage the Beatitudes as poetry and as prophetic. Her stirring rendition is a hopeful light as she shows us how God's dream is *the* way to see the world in all its beauty and heartache, and she invites us to the kind of loving and living that is a gift. Through the stories of her family's life together, their journey together, I understand blessing in a new way, in flesh-and-blood ways, skin-and-bones ways, tears-and-laughter ways—where our blessedness is not only a wonder but good and true."

—**Mihee Kim-Kort**, author of *Outside the Lines: How Embracing Queerness Will Transform Your Faith*; co-pastor of First Presbyterian Church, Annapolis, Maryland

Blessed
Are the
Rest
of Us

Blessed Are the Rest of Us

HOW LIMITS AND LONGING MAKE US WHOLE

Micha Boyett

Brazos Press

a division of Baker Publishing Group
Grand Rapids, Michigan

Published by Brazos Press
a division of Baker Publishing Group
Grand Rapids, Michigan
BrazosPress.com

Printed in the United States of America

Library of Congress Cataloging-in-Publication Data
Names: Boyett, Micha, author.
Title: Blessed are the rest of us : how limits and longing make us whole / Micha
    Boyett.
Description: Grand Rapids, Michigan : Brazos Press, a division of Baker
    Publishing Group, [2024] | Includes bibliographical references.
Identifiers: LCCN 2023035302 | ISBN 9781587436093 (paperback) | ISBN
    9781587436291 (casebound) | ISBN 9781493445004 (ebook)
Subjects: LCSH: Gratitude—Religious aspects—Christianity. | Beatitudes. |
    Christian life—Study and teaching.
Classification: LCC BV4647.G8 B68 2024 | DDC 241/.4—dc23/eng/20230912
LC record available at https://lccn.loc.gov/2023035302

Some names and details have been changed to protect the privacy of the individuals involved.

The excerpt from the poem "We Are Surprised" by Ada Limón is from *Bright
Dead Things*. Copyright © 2015 by Ada Limón. Reprinted with the permission of
The Permissions Company, LLC on behalf of Milkweed Editions, milkweed.org.

The excerpt from poem "XXIX" by Rainer Maria Rilke and translated by Anita
Barrows and Joanna Macy is from *In Praise of Mortality*. Copyright 2005, 2016
by Anita Barrows and Joanna Macy. Reprinted with the permission of Echo Point
Books & Media, echopointbooks.com.

The author is represented by the literary agency of The Zoë Pagnamenta Agency.

Baker Publishing Group publications use paper produced from sustainable for-
estry practices and postconsumer waste whenever possible.

24 25 26 27 28 29 30   7 6 5 4 3 2 1

For August, Brooks, and Ace,
dreams of God coming true

Here it is:
the new way of living with the world

inside of us so we cannot lose it,
and we cannot be lost.

—Ada Limón, "We Are Surprised"

CONTENTS

NOTE FROM THE AUTHOR

In 2006, I took a two-week course on the life of Christ with Frederick Dale Bruner, author of a two-volume commentary on the gospel of Matthew. He was sharp, humble, and winsome, and his teaching planted a seed in me that has grown into a deep and abiding love for the Beatitudes, which eventually shaped this book.

Stephanie Spellers's book *The Church Cracked Open*, along with her understanding of the dream of God and beloved community, opened something new in me and offered me new language for the vision Jesus offers in Matthew 5.

Mark Scandrette's *The Ninefold Path of Jesus* was incredibly valuable for helping me form the practical bones of this book. And, finally, Jonathan T. Pennington's scholarly work *The Sermon on the Mount and Human Flourishing* gave me the language for a book about the mysterious nearness of God in our limits and longings that brings us into whole and flourishing life.

This book explores issues of justice as it relates to disability as well as how it pertains to race and sexuality. I tell my story as the mom of an autistic child with Down syndrome, and in doing so, I hope to honor my son and the greater disability community.

I acknowledge, though, that language can evolve, and the way we speak about issues of race, sexuality, or ability may change over time. I've attempted to be fully authentic with my own story and careful with the language I use to describe my son's experience of the world, while seeking out sensitivity readers to offer early feedback. I take responsibility for any failure of language that may not honor any group of people, particularly groups to which I don't belong. Writing nonfiction can feel like a fumble toward the truth. I'm grateful for grace in the process.

All personal narratives are told as I remember to the best of my ability. I do my best to present the heart of those conversations, though I can't guarantee their accuracy word for word. The quotes from Nadia Bolz-Weber's sermon are taken straight from a written narrative she was kind enough to share with me. All stories of friends and family have been told with their permission, though some names have been changed to protect privacy.

Macarism: *Greek. Noun. A compelling proclamation that expresses a blessing. An exhortation to live a particular way. A congratulation to specific persons in specific conditions.*

Makarioi: *Greek. Adjective, plural. Wise. True. Whole. Flourishing.*

A Poem by Jesus of Nazareth[*]

Makarioi are the weak ones, the poor in wealth and the poor in soul. They are caretakers of the dream of God.

Makarioi are the ones who grieve. They will be invited to a divine banquet.

Makarioi are the powerless ones and the ones who release their power. They will recognize that the entire earth has always been theirs.

Makarioi are the ones who long for justice that restores and dignifies. They will be filled with whole and mutually dependent love.

Makarioi are the ones who give mercy. They will receive in turn what they have offered in love.

Makarioi are the true ones. They will have eyes to see the Spirit of Truth.

Makarioi are the ones who serve peace. They will be called kin, safe in God's chosen family.

Makarioi are the ones who suffer for doing good. Their dreams will become like God's dream.

Makarioi are the fearless ones, the rejected or pushed out. They will find joy on the edges, coworking with God, transforming the world in love.

---

[*] This is my own rendering of the Beatitudes. The definition of *macarism* comes from Dale Bruner, *Matthew: A Commentary* (Grand Rapids: Eerdmans, 2004), 159.

PROLOGUE

The Dream of God

When he saw the crowds he ascended the mountain. And when he sat down his disciples came to him. And he opened his mouth and taught them. —Matthew 5:1–2[1]

I walk the length of Grace Cathedral holding a candle and wearing a white acolyte robe, hardly the religious garb of my adult churchgoing life. I pass by the faces of fellow conference-goers. This weekend I taught a small seminar on the spirituality of rest, and now I find myself leading this processional with the other speakers trailing along. I climb the stairs toward the altar and do my best to steady the candle into its brass votive stand. Then I find a seat among the others, who are settling into the choir stalls beside me. The ceiling rises high into dark Gothic angles, surrounded on all sides by early twentieth-century stained-glass images of Jesus's ministry.

This is the last act of a beautiful weekend, during which people from all sorts of backgrounds—artists and speakers, theologians and writers—have told their stories of why they remain believers in the radical and inefficient Jesus. And how, despite our separation from the mainstream politics of American Christianity, despite the sex scandals and power grabbing of so many American Christian leaders, we are all still clinging to a faith revealed through the exceptional life of an ancient traveling rabbi who invited his followers to imagine a new way to God.

Nadia Bolz-Weber approaches the lectern to send us off. She stands at the center of the raised stage, just to the side of our crew of speakers, wearing the traditional robe of a high-church minister, white cloth tied in a bunch at the waist with a rope. The next time I hear her preach, six weeks later in Chattanooga, Tennessee, she will be shaken and deeply grieved at the funeral of her friend and conference collaborator, Rachel Held Evans. But at this moment, Rachel is sitting behind me, vibrant. And Nadia's voice is light. She is jubilant, bringing a successful conference to a close. She reads the week's gospel passage aloud.

The passage is from John, chapter 12: the story of Mary, the sister of Lazarus, breaking a jar of pure nard on the feet of Jesus. I listen as Nadia sets the scene, imagining Lazarus, newly raised from the dead, reclining beside his teacher, Jesus. The passage tells the story of Martha serving the meal, while Mary offers Jesus her most valuable possession, an unbroken jar of perfume, something likely intended for an intimate marital ceremony. Mary disrupts cultural expectations and breaks open that valuable jar of nard oil right there during the men's dinner. She chooses to honor Jesus, despite the taboo, the judgments, and the whispers she would elicit. She honors him because she loves him.

Nadia points us to Lazarus, the quiet brother of Mary, sitting right there at the table next to Jesus. She is fascinated with Lazarus, who has barely scrubbed the stench of his own death off his body in the narrative before this one. In John 12, he is sitting at the side of the one who had miraculously pulled him out of the death gravity that we humans have spent all our existence resisting.

Nadia wonders about this man. Of all the people Jesus could have brought back to life, what made this one special? Why did Jesus choose Lazarus? Surely Jesus had encountered other deaths among the throngs of people begging him to bring his miracle powers their way. He'd been walking the countryside with his disciples and followers, coating blind eyes with mud and opening them up, sealing the broken flesh of lepers excluded by society's cultural and social norms. He practiced the kind of loving touch that imparted dignity to those whose bodies refused to fit into societal norms.[2] But this? A dead man who had already spent three days entombed and decomposing? There were dead people everywhere in the world every day. Why, of all the dead, did Lazarus deserve Jesus's tears first and his God magic after?

Nadia quotes her friend, Scottish pastor and scholar Doug Gay, whom she had heard preach about Lazarus once before. He wondered why Lazarus, despite having so much written about him, never says a word in the scriptures, "not when he stumbles out of his tomb and not at this macabre little dinner party."

While Nadia speaks, I spin my wedding ring in a circle, using only my left thumb and pinky, around and around. My thumb reaches the top of the diamond that once belonged to my husband's great-grandmother, long before he lived, before he and I would meet, marry, have August, then Brooks, and eventually our youngest son, Ace.

"So my friend Doug wondered if perhaps Lazarus couldn't speak," she says. I think of my two older babies and their earliest words, how Brooks used to waddle bare legged and diapered, dragging the stuffed pup he called "Gawgy." Speaking can sometimes feel like everything. It allows us to define ourselves, make ourselves knowable. If we can't explain ourselves to the world, we lose control over the narrative of our lives. Can those among us who are silent ever be fully known?

"Maybe the one whom Jesus loved, maybe the one person we know Jesus cried over," Nadia continues, "maybe the one person Jesus deemed so valuable that he would not allow death to take him: maybe this one person wasn't verbal."

I squirm a little in my seat. My heart picks up a quicker rhythm. *Nonverbal* is a word I know deeply but haven't been using to describe my youngest son. Ace, four years old, plays in his own world at school, doesn't get invited to the preschool birthday parties, and doesn't say hi when old ladies stop us on the street to comment on his cuteness. *Nonverbal* isn't a term I throw around. In fact, it is a term I mostly avoid. When I describe Ace, I say, "He doesn't talk much, but he's working on it!" I've been too afraid to use it, afraid it will forever seal the door, forever prove to the world—and to him—that he will never speak. But here I am, listening to this sermon, mother of a boy who at four years old still doesn't call me mama. Nonverbal.

Nadia keeps going. "My friend Doug asked, 'What if Lazarus was Mary and Martha's wee brother with Down syndrome?'"

It's a kick in the gut, really. I stare at my hands, my knee bouncing in my seat, half expecting Nadia to turn and face me, terrified that all four hundred people at the conference will shift their faces toward me, like in some creepy zombie movie, as if they know my story, my kid's story. I raise my eyes from my hands to the congregation as slowly as I can. All faces are on Nadia, not me.

Her voice slows, and I feel the impossibility of the story she's telling. Does she know she is talking about my boy? Does she know how deeply I understand what it is to carry on long, sweet conversations with a child who never talks back? Lazarus, I remind myself. This is about Lazarus. But also, she's talking about my boy. She is preaching that he and Lazarus are the same. Lazarus, the one human so important, so significant, that the biblical Messiah sobs at his grave, that his sisters demand Jesus save him. I know, more fully than Nadia can know, more fully than those who sit beside me in robes in the speakers' section, the grief and delight of loving Lazarus. And there, in the nave at Grace Cathedral, under the stained glass and in a white, ancient-looking robe, I imagine Jesus standing at my four-year-old son's grave, weeping for my child.

"What if Lazarus was Mary and Martha's wee brother with Down syndrome?" Nadia pauses after her words, and I hold all my fear and my love and my hope in that moment. Could it be possible that the most important person in Jesus's life—his dearest friend, the one he chose to return to the living—might just be the one everyone else deemed least worthy of that gift? Could Lazarus share the same face as my son?

Nadia continues, "It just seems totally true to me given everything I know about Jesus, . . . [who] walked around like he definitely didn't understand the rules, like he didn't understand who supposedly mattered and who supposedly didn't."

* * *

Who matters? That's the question I'd been asking in the years since I answered a call from the genetic counselor four months into my pregnancy with Ace. We lived in San Francisco, and I had been pushing Brooks in a stroller from my parking space a few blocks from his gymnastics class. The voice on the phone was young and cheerful and spoke my name as if she were a barista calling for me in a crowded café.

I had given birth to two healthy little boys before that pregnancy. My older kids were developing as expected—strong, both in the ninety-fifth percentile in height, both good eaters and early talkers. I had no reason to think my third baby would be any different. I was thirty-five and healthy. My husband and I had hoped my twenty-week ultrasound would reveal that this time around it was a girl. It had to be—the pregnancy had felt exceptional, distinctive.

It turns out the baby was a boy and the pregnancy was "remarkable" (the word in a recent assessment report from our current school district used to describe Ace's diagnosis). That's not the word the doctor had used two weeks earlier when he showed us the calcium deposit in our baby's heart, a common physical marker for Down syndrome. Still, based on my age, this child had only a 1 in 476 chance of carrying the extra twenty-first chromosome that characterizes the genetic condition. It was unlikely, the doctor had said. I had some blood work done to rule it out, to give me peace of mind for the rest of the pregnancy.

I had been expecting the geneticist to confirm my suspicions: *Nothing unusual here. No reason to worry.* I pushed the stroller around the big tree that bulged up the sidewalk near Lincoln Avenue. Brooks rocked back and forth to the awkward lift and shove of the stroller. I held the phone in place, my head tilted right to squeeze it against my shoulder. I remember making it to the crosswalk, pausing to wait for the light, looking down to see my toddler's eyes locked on the cars moving past us. "We got your blood test results back," she said. Then she used the word *positive*. "The test came back positive." That word clanged around in my skull begging for clarification. *Positive*, the word we use for good news, cheery souls, kindhearted dog training. The test came back positive, she said. And the light changed. I wiggled the stroller off the curb while I mentally unraveled and reordered her word, neurons firing in every direction. Positive, positive, positive.

She said there was a 99.7 percent chance that my child would have Down syndrome. I stepped into the street. "Okay," I said. "Okay." I walked into the park, past the hollow log August and Brooks always crawled through, past the community garden, the old stadium on Frederick Street. I ended the call and slipped my phone into my pocket. The sky hardened and slanted, pressing in, tunneling me.

* * *

By the time Nadia preached that night in San Francisco, my "remarkable" pregnancy had turned into a blond, blue-eyed, tiny-glasses-wearing little boy, a four-year-old who didn't speak. He was the size of a two-year-old and had passed the stage when it was still acceptable for us to pull out a diaper in public and call it normal. And at the time of the conference, in spring 2019, he was showing signs of autism, a diagnosis I had been terrified to pursue, as if naming his unique experience of the world might silence his voice forever.

That night at Grace Cathedral, Nadia's words soar toward me like wild seeds, pressing themselves in the center of my chest, a planting for a future sturdy hope. Jesus, she is saying, lived out his inefficient view of the world—the conviction of who matters, who wins, whose life is most valuable—in his very friendships.

His miraculous power gave back life to the nonspeaking brother of Mary and Martha, new life for the one he loved, his friend, who had Down syndrome. My chest tells me to wait. Something good will grow right there, in the soft center of me.

Whether or not it's a fact that the man Jesus chose to raise from the dead shared my son's intellectual disability, Nadia's voice radiates with the fierce delight of the idea. "My Christian faith," she says, "tells me that this is the most true thing I have ever heard."

The most true thing. Of course, I think, of course. That's what I've been trying to say about God; that's what I've been wanting to write all these years since my youngest son arrived and I struggled to find words to explain his goodness to a world that continually questions his worth. I have been wanting to say that he is uniquely valuable. Even *blessed*.

. . .

This is a book about a poem, a poem that speaks to the question of what it means to be blessed, a poem uttered before a sermon, almost as a riff, spilling from the lips of a barely known spiritual teacher in the beginning of his ministry to a crowd of farmers and fishers on a hillside.

Jesus of Nazareth had already caused a commotion when he was baptized by the unruly and eccentric John the Baptist along the banks of the Jordan River. His emergence from John's baptismal waters had blown a hole in the atmospheric divide between heaven and earth. The divine one's voice slipped through the veil and into the ears of anyone who stood close enough to hear what was spoken from that other realm: "This is my Son." *Pay attention to him.*

After his baptism, an intensive season of fasting in the wilderness, and the arrest of John, Jesus had packed up, left his hometown of Nazareth, and arrived in the bustling seaside city of Capernaum. His presence alone seemed to draw strangers into his vicinity, inviting people to a religious movement they surely didn't know how to name. He had convinced a few vagabonds to leave their day jobs and join him in a mission that would eventually include telling stories to crowds on hills and near bodies of water, encountering many ordinary folks needing healing, and performing some wild miracles that would leave his followers stunned. All of this would lead to a confusing and violent end with a profound and unexpected postscript.[3]

Some scholars place the setting of Jesus's longest sermon on the grassy side of the Korazim Plateau, just a walk away from Capernaum.[4] As he sat before his followers on that hill, before teaching what would later be called "The Sermon on the Mount," Jesus offered a poem—a litany of blessings that followed the structure of the Greco-Roman virtue poets of his day.[5] This poem, eventually known as the Beatitudes,[6] was a touchstone, a concise declaration of his values and purpose, a preface to the message that would eventually serve as the foundational moral teaching of Christianity.

This is a book about that preface and what it reveals to us about human value, how we find our identity, and who deserves honor. It's a book exploring what it means to be *blessed*, that overused, often trite, hashtag of a religious word no one ever really knows how to define, a word I recently found stitched into cotton pajamas on the rack in TJ Maxx, an adjective that some biblical scholars translate from the original Greek word *makarioi* as "happy," "favored," or even "flourishing."[7] *Blessed* is the word Jesus assigns to the weak, the weary, and the worn out. In a world that lived, and still lives, by a script that honors those who wield power, who live with ease, and who need not rely on relationships to survive, this little poem offers an entirely different perspective.[8] This poem is how Jesus chose to answer the mysterious and seemingly eternal question of human happiness. It's a revolutionary reimagining of authentic community[9] in the form of provocations and surprising promises.[10] As Jesus began his sermon, he played the role of both prophet and poet, inviting his listeners to a new way of being in the world, a way that would lead to both individual and communal transformation.

The crowd that gathered around Jesus that day was hardly full of winners. The stories we find in the gospels reveal that Jesus seems to have first attracted his own social class: blue-collar workers just trying to earn enough to provide for the little ones and keep the roof from leaking. Maybe that's why they skipped out on work for the day, stretched themselves out on scratchy grass and rocky soil, and made the most of the sunshine, curious enough to show up for a makeshift religious experience. There must have been some vibrant sparkle to Jesus, something that caused folks to follow him up that hill and tune in to his longest recorded sermon.[11]

Those who listened to his teaching surely had arrived with their own cultural understanding of how God acted in the world.[12] The world was made of haves and have-nots, and an almighty power in the sky blasted some and bestowed riches and comfort on others. I imagine that those ancient god-in-the-sky beliefs probably weren't too far from those of many North American Christians—we who spin colorful screens with our pointer fingers, scrolling through hashtag-blessed Facebook posts and finely curated Instagram feeds of happy, healthy, straight-A-earning children, three-car garages, and successful business ventures. The working class of ancient Palestine who lived with the wretched reality of Roman occupation couldn't possibly be blessed, their lives full of daily reminders that they must be far from the honor bestowed by the divine.

Maybe that's why they were there. With little freedom, Roman soldiers on their streets, and an outside empire that taxed what little income their day trade brought in, they might have hoped this religious leader would instigate a military force that could finally reckon with the oppressive power in their midst, crush the Roman forces that tyrannized their daily lives. Maybe whatever charisma Jesus had going for him ignited in the crowd an old hope for a leader who might restore Israel to the great nation once ruled by King David.

Or maybe they weren't thinking about military power at all. Maybe they simply wanted to hear something new. When folks are bold enough to sit on the grass to hear an unapproved spiritual teacher interpret their scriptures, they tend to be hungry for something more than the old story of "the rich and the powerful must be important because they got what everyone else wants." This crowd had lived a script that said blessing was equated with empire, wealth, and ease. Jesus was there to take their old script of what it meant to be human and toss it.[13]

So he started with a poem of macarisms, a speaking device from the Greco-Roman virtue tradition that would have been very familiar to his audience.[14] In that tradition, a teacher listed, based on observation, ways of being in the world that would produce happiness or authentic human flourishing. Jesus delivered an unexpected list, one that spoke intimately to his listeners' daily struggles as oppressed people in a brutal empire. Those who practice wisdom. Those who will experience true and whole life. The ones who will flourish. "Wise, true, and whole," Jesus said, "are the ones who suffer, the ones who have no power, the ones who are mistreated." And so he began his ministry, inviting his listeners to use their spiritual imagination to reorder their notions of society, prioritizing the vulnerable above the powerful.

As he did so, Jesus used a phrase he would repeat throughout his ministry: the kingdom of God. It was the nucleus of his teaching, the central metaphor he used to explain the spiritual power, holy generosity, and sacred connection making its way into the world. The kingdom of God, or the reign of God, helped his listeners reimagine the divine at work among them, opening up a new way of being right there in the middle of their ordinary, not-so-easy lives. This kingdom, he taught, was beyond human modes of power, violence, and tribal division. This kingdom would change everything, because it challenged notions of who was in or out, who got to claim the blessing of God, who had the honor of calling themselves important.[15]

In the kingdom Jesus spoke of, true communion with God provides ordinary people with a different and beautiful way of being human—a way of justice, peace, and inclusion, a way that removes our natural inclinations to divide and defend and instead turns us toward one another. It's a way that just might shake the systems of the world like a snow globe, releasing what has always lived on the bottom into the wild equality of the upside down, a way in which the powerful and the weak are equally necessary to the flourishing of everything.

Jesus used the word *kingdom* because that's how his listeners understood reality. If their safety, health, and sustenance were controlled by whatever empire reigned, then he wanted them to imagine a world where a divine love was in charge, where every part of their lives pulsed around that love, even as their hardscrabble daily existence was dictated by violence and oppression. Perhaps today we don't need that metaphor of "kingdom" in a culture in which our royalty looks more like celebrity, in which the system of democracy, while still overwhelmed by powermongers, provides us with notions of control over who rules us, something those listening to Jesus's sermon could not have lived or known. Most of us don't relate to a society ruled in the way Jesus's audience would have understood it. But we do know that there is endless pain and suffering because of the misuse of power, because we humans are endlessly self-centered and attached to hoarding power for ourselves.

Author and Episcopal priest Stephanie Spellers suggests that instead of imagining a kingdom, a better way for us to understand what Jesus had in mind when he spoke of this script, this new way of living in the world, is to imagine "the dream of God."[16] What Jesus calls the kingdom of God is the dream that exists in the imagination of the divine. It's the intention of God, the original hope for creation, and the ultimate reality for those of us willing to move our imaginations and intentions toward justice, peace, and inclusion, with the help of a divine love that propels us forward.

Richard Rohr uses the phrase the "really real" to communicate the same notion.[17] In this world where systems of oppression sell us lies about our own value, about what it means to be human, God continues to point us toward ultimate truth, the truth Jesus calls God's kingdom. This ultimate truth is our invitation to live lives of meaning, joy, and participation in the restoration of all things. It's an invitation to allow the inclusive love of God to be the center of our orbits, drawing us in, keeping us in rotation around what's most true, so that we can reform our distorted vision of power grabbing, our propensity for both internal and external habits of abuse, and our inclination to look past those who wield the least amount of power in this world. Jesus was restructuring more than his listeners' social dogmas. He was restructuring their personal visions of what it meant to flourish. He was presenting a new vision of life as it is meant to be lived: in a community, whole and healthy, where those with the least power are given priority and honor. In this dream God is dreaming for the world, Jesus told the crowd, the ones who will receive the highest levels of honor are never the ones we would expect.

On that hill, surrounded by a crowd that may or may not have been tracking with these wild ideas about God, Jesus recited a radical litany of blessings, all of which have nothing to do with being good. He listed nine human experiences of suffering, generosity, and longing, then he pronounced blessings. He blessed those who have known what it is to be weak, to grieve, or to hope for a better world, calling them favored, whole, and drawn into the holy gravitational orbit of love. The ones who flourish, Jesus said, are the weak, the broken, the beat-up, and the burned-out. The blessed ones end up on top when the snow globe is turned over and everything is shaken up.

The Beatitudes, this poem that prefaces the Sermon on the Mount, still confuses and delights many of us coming to it two thousand years later. There's no pep talk, no appeal to the people in power, no how-tos, no easy steps toward spiritual revelation. Instead, the words of Jesus are sad, focused on the weak and the poor and the broken.

But if we embrace his vision, his poem offers us a new script, a new way of being human. Jesus reveals the really real underneath what we think we know about God and what we think we know about the world. His poem tells us that there is a dream that belongs to the divine one, and it's a dream about blessing. And in the dream of God, blessing is rarely what we think it is.

• • •

The night Nadia preached, I understood that something transformative had been sowed in the center of me, wild seeds of hope pressed deep, promising to sink their roots into something true and good. Was Jesus dear friends with a nonspeaking man who had Down syndrome? And was this his way of living out the value system he presented in the Beatitudes? What if the dream of God was manifested in his love and privileging of Lazarus above all others? Lazarus, newly risen, next to Jesus at the table, silent except for the musical "aahs" he made when Martha presented his favorite meal, flapping his hands with joy when Jesus told a funny story?

What if that man—my son—was the most important of all of us, the one whose life most needed to be given back?

I left Grace Cathedral knowing, more deeply than I ever had, that loving my child was going to break my heart and that the brokenness would be my healing. I had lived most of my life striving to be worthy of blessing, longing to earn my value through performance, goodness, and hard work. But like Jesus's first listeners, like Lazarus, maybe my script was being rewritten. What if, like Lazarus, like Ace, my value would be found in love, in my silence, and perhaps in the grave?

I imagine the rich baritone of Jesus's voice calling his friend by name from the dark tomb. I picture divine love surging its power into Lazarus's still heart, where it contracts and expands in a living rhythm that restores life back into his cold body and lifeless limbs. Outside the tomb, Jesus welcomed his least-likely friend into the sort of blessing I've spent my life longing to receive. He called his name: "Ace! Ace! Come forth, my friend."

But maybe he was also calling me. *Micha! You too; you come out too.*

1

For the Weak Ones

Makarioi are the weak ones, the poor in wealth and the poor in soul. They are caretakers of the dream of God.

FEBRUARY 2016 (ACE, TEN MONTHS OLD)
SAN FRANCISCO

In my imagination, the breeze lifts off the Sea of Galilee, providing Jesus a brief respite from the heat of the day as he hikes two hours to the south. When he and the crowd that has gathered arrive at an open space, he finds a seat on the slope where folks can see him, hear his voice as they sit cross-legged or stretch out on their sides on the prickly grass. Maybe a crew of kids runs in a meadow somewhere below the adults.

This is the image that comes to mind at 6:00 a.m. while I practice what some of my favorite spiritual writers call imaginative prayer. Chris is making my coffee, so I have around eight minutes—his coffee making is a science—before he sits beside me, cup in hand, and we catch up. This is my moment to pray.

Maybe this is Jesus's first sermon. If it is, I wonder if he feels ready. I wonder how long these ideas have been forming in his mind. I wonder if he changed his plan when he saw the reality of those who gathered before him. More than once, the gospel writer Matthew notes that Jesus was moved with compassion for the crowds.[1] Maybe at the base of his ribs a flame begins to glow at the sight of them. Every prophetic word spoken over him, every conversation about purpose, every moment of *knowing* that sparked his imagination when he heard the Hebrew scriptures read aloud in the synagogue—these are becoming real. All of it has led to this moment.

"His disciples came to him, and he began to teach them. He said: 'Blessed are the poor in spirit, for theirs is the kingdom of heaven.'" Jesus sits on a rock where the path slopes upward. His voice carries downhill toward the crowd.

The New Testament offers two versions of Jesus's most famous sermon and two versions of the macarisms that Jesus recites just before he preaches.[2] In Matthew's version of this sermon, Jesus begins his poem with a blessing for those who live with poverty of spirit, "the spiritual zeros, the spiritually bankrupt."[3] In Luke's version, Jesus speaks these words in a completely different setting. He's standing on a plain, and his poem consists of only four blessings, followed by four woes. Some scholars believe these divergent accounts suggest that Jesus might have given this sermon more than once, in different places. In Luke's recounting, Jesus's language is centered on physical experience. In both accounts, he uses the same word for poverty, *ptōchoi*, the Greek word we translate as "poor." This *poor* didn't refer to the 80 percent of those in the lower middle class in ancient Palestine, many of whom lived a hard-scrabble life and struggled to make ends meet under the oppressive Roman regime.[4] This word meant the poorest of the poor, the ones deemed unnecessary to society, the rejected.[5] Unlike in Luke's version, in which the blessing falls solely on those who live in physical poverty, Matthew's version refers to a kind of spiritual poverty.

Which does Jesus intend—a blessing for the materially poor or the spiritually poor? If he meant to bless only the physically and economically poor, then Jesus's blessing could almost appear cruel. For those who live in extreme poverty, plagued by hunger, disease, and often abuse at the hands of a culture that has rejected their humanity, Jesus's words seem to spiritualize their pain.[6]

Maybe Luke's telling of the story doesn't allow his readers the full picture we find in Matthew, which offers a counterbalance. When we come to this first beatitude, we're invited to incorporate both the spiritual emphasis of Matthew's text and the social reality of Luke's. When we read them in tandem, perhaps we get a fuller grasp of Jesus's intention, the experience of two eyes working together.[7]

God's special attention and honor, Jesus says, belong to the impoverished, those who lack the physical stability and comfort needed for safety and health in this world. And they also belong to the impoverished of spirit, those who lack healthy and whole souls, who suffer under layers of human emotional and spiritual pain. In Matthew's translation, we find language that points to blessings on those who *feel* their poverty. To the physically *ptōchoi* and the spiritually *ptōchoi*, Jesus is making a promise: I am here, and I am bringing a whole and flourishing life, especially for you.[8]

• • •

"Hey." I open my eyes to find Chris's hand extending a cup of coffee in my direction. I take it, and he sits beside me in the dim light of the living room.

"Hey," I say. "What do you think it means to be blessed?"

Early morning is the only time we're able to connect these days. Of the twelve years we've been married, we've spent the past four practicing this ritual. We'd both say that these quiet minutes every morning have formed our relationship more deeply than any date night or marriage book we've picked up. Our early morning conversations—while we sit side-by-side, drinking Chris's ever-improving experiments in pour-over and Chemex coffee, reading, praying, and wrestling with what we believe— have become the heartbeat of our relationship. We wake and steady ourselves in each other's presence before the day drags us into its chaos.

Maybe Chris is surprised I'm talking about scripture. Throughout the past six years, I have slowly left my former way of being a Christian, with the certainties and cultural expectations baked into the evangelical faith. And in doing so, I've left behind the homework-style Bible studies and long list of prayer demands I'd once pressured myself to work through. Now I read spiritual books or simply sit in silence. Or, as I'm doing now, I find myself holding up a word that's prominent in the subculture I've rejected, gazing on it like an artifact. What do I believe? How do I want to talk about God?

The word *blessed* has been among the vocabulary I've removed from my daily life. In the faith of my young adulthood, it was a word that filled my conversations: a term to close out emails or to describe a pay raise. I had heard it claimed by the wealthy, the healthy, or those who generally had good things coming their way. It was a spiritually rosy-coated notion that the harder you prayed, the more likely God would fix the universe in your favor—an equation that faith plus persistence would equal change. I stopped believing that a long time ago.

"When you say blessed, what do you mean?" Chris asks.

"I'm thinking about when Jesus gives blessings in the Beatitudes. I mean, he's obviously not fixing anybody's problems, right? He tells the poor in spirit they're blessed, and then what happens? They go home?"

This season of my life will be one I'll look back on with tenderness. I'll learn to honor the version of me that juggled not only those early mornings but also the exhaustive list of therapists and specialists. I cart Ace to his appointments in the afternoons, help the older boys scribble their homework in waiting rooms, and trek thirty minutes across the city during rush hour back to our rental house in the Sunset District, where the task of creating dinner from whatever exists in our fridge awaits me. By the time Chris gets home each night around 7:00 p.m., I feel wobbly. Not simply tired but unsteady, as if I'm living someone else's life, moving from one child's intense need to another's. Sometimes I catch a glimpse of my face in the mirror and remind myself that I'm still there. *Hi, Micha.*

When I ask this question, having just imagined the moment of Jesus on the hill giving his blessings to a crowd of weary, ordinary people, Chris knows I'm on the hunt for some kind of answer. But he's not sure what I'm getting at.

It's been almost a year since Ace showed up. His arrival shook us, opened cracks in each of us we hadn't seen before. As we've loved and raised a child whose needs have required more time, money, and energy, we've also experienced a shared electric current of anxiety. Parenting Ace has revealed the rawest parts of ourselves—fears, failures, and weaknesses that would probably have shown themselves at some point in our lives together. But Ace's presence has sped us toward the kind of vulnerability that arrives only alongside struggle. Desperation has a way of taking us further down and further out, beyond what we thought had been our edges.[9]

The vulnerability that lives on the other side of our deep fears can shake up the whole system. Later on, we will sit in a therapist's office together, peeling back layers of hardened and practiced ego that neither of us had needed to acknowledge until then. We will learn to be kind to each other, in a way that will feel more real than the sweetness that existed when our life together was easier. We will learn to love each other at the bottom of our anxiety and sadness and need. Chris will become a kind of miracle to me, my steadfast companion in a life that feels increasingly frantic.

"Okay." Chris smiles. "So you're asking if Jesus was full of crap when he gave the Beatitudes?"

I laugh. "No!" Then I raise my eyebrows. "Maybe."

I want to say something to Chris about why this passage keeps showing up in my mind when I try to pray. I want to say that I'm desperate for a Jesus promise that can calm the life Chris and I are making together. Right now, Ace is losing weight, our oldest child, August, pushes back on every boundary we set, and Brooks is being dragged along for the ride. And though I don't know how to survive this season of my life, I find myself turning to Jesus's teachings in the Beatitudes as a kind of anchor. I want to be blessed. I want whatever this life is that I'm living to be *good*.

"I've just been thinking about Jesus blessing the poor in spirit and how . . . I don't know. I guess I feel . . . spiritually weak." I don't need to say that Ace's life has pulled me back to the teachings of Jesus, how Ace's challenges feel like more than I can hold. Chris knows this. He probably also knows I like the idea that when Jesus kick-started his entire ministry, he began by pronouncing that the good life actually belongs to the ones who will never be good enough.[10] I take a sip of my coffee, watching the steam rise toward my face. "I'm pretty sure I'm poor in spirit."

Chris leans forward on the couch, elbows on his knees, coffee cupped in both his hands. He turns toward me, his hair tousled and thinning a little on top. There are bits of gray starting to show in his facial hair. But his eyes are still as blue as they were when we met fourteen years ago, the same year I gave him the rumpled pale-blue and red-heart pajama pants he's currently wearing. I'm amazed they're intact, though they're still too short for his long legs.

"Is that what you were praying about?" He looks at me, gentleness in his face. He sees what this season has demanded of me, of both of us.

"I was imagining Jesus giving his blessings, and I was about to get to the part where he blesses me." I smile and take another sip of coffee. I want to believe that God has a dream for me that is richer and deeper than Lexapro-controlled child-rearing.

Chris smiles at me. "And you want to know what it is to be blessed."

"What I want," I say, "is to find out that all along blessing has been more than sentimentality. Because if that's all it is, I'm not interested." I think about the mark of the cross I make on my boys' foreheads every night before bed, "sharing in God's audacity," as Barbara Brown Taylor writes, calling the ordinary remarkable.[11] That's what I want blessing to be—the audacity of God, something remarkable. I want blessing that doesn't exist for my own inspiration. I want blessing that's *real*.

Yesterday, I found Brooks holding Ace in the rocking chair beside my bed, singing the song he, August, and I had written for their baby brother: "I am Acey! I am Acey! I'm a sweet little boy. I am Acey! I am Acey! And I bring so much joy." Ace had been crying, but Brooks, in his kindergarten-sized lap, held his brother like a ragdoll, rocking him, shushing like I do to the beat of the rocking chair. "Sh, sh, sh," Brooks said. The moment felt holy. *Blessed?* Was Brooks sharing God's audacity?

There is something in Taylor's phrase, like a secret code I'm invited to decipher. And if I discover the hidden wisdom, perhaps it will invite me into God's audacity—a blessing beyond the shallow promises of a world that sees Ace, with his disability, as somehow half angel, half human, here to teach us all Hallmark-style what life is about. God's audacity points to a blessing bigger than saccharine stereotypes. I want to honor how hard this first year with Ace has felt and at the same time experience his value acknowledged. I want the really real.

"I just mean," I say looking at Chris, knowing it's almost time to wake the kids and start this day, "that Jesus used this list to create his whole thing, his whole ministry. And he starts with the poor in spirit. He starts with Ace."

Chris takes one last sip of his coffee, still looking at me. "And maybe he starts with you?"

"Maybe."

We sit in silence for a beat.

"What was that phrase you were thinking about the other day, about the way Jesus blessed people?"

"Oh." I smile. "Liberal and excessive," I say, not remembering whether I read that phrase or if I made it up myself. "Jesus was liberal and excessive with his blessings."

"That's the thing," he says. Then he stands up. It's time.

•　•　•

"Dinosaur eggs!"

"Dinosaur eggs, *please, Mama,*" I correct Brooks, who sits beside August in the kitchen, fifteen minutes after the end of our coffee time on the couch. It's 6:45 a.m., and both my kindergartener and my third grader are waiting for me to make some breakfast magic happen. I grab the eggs from the fridge.

"I want pancakes. Daddy promised pancakes."

"Aug, Daddy is getting ready. He can't make pancakes this morning." I hear Chris's shower running in the background of this early morning ritual. Ace is in his high chair. I've sprinkled Cheerios onto his tray in hopes he'll get his chunky fist around one of them and lift it to his mouth. But I'm doubtful. The sooner his big brothers start eating, the more likely he can actually eat. He needs attention, a hand to lift one slow spoonful at a time to his mouth. I don't have time right now to lift any spoonfuls to any person's mouth.

"Daddy promised pancakes!" August turns on his angry voice. I feel my heart pick up speed.

"I wasn't there when Dad promised pancakes, Aug. I don't know about pancakes. But I can make you a dinosaur egg or a bagel." He is on the edge. I can tell. And if I find out from Chris that last night before bed he promised our sleepy eight-year-old there would be pancakes on a Tuesday morning at 6:45 when we have to leave the house by 7:25, I will make him pay me back for this pain in the form of chocolate milkshakes and foot massages, for as long as I decide is necessary.

August kicks his feet against the cabinets under the counter, and I ignore him, gathering a slice of bread and pulling an egg from the carton. Chris and his dad renamed egg-in-a-hole "dinosaur eggs" thirty years ago, a tradition we keep. "Do you hear me?" August yells.

"August." I breathe to keep my cool. "I hear you." I try to remember what our child therapist has taught me. I need to acknowledge his desires and still set clear boundaries. "You want pancakes. You think Daddy promised to make pancakes . . ."

"He *did* promise pancakes!" he interrupts me.

"You say Daddy promised pancakes, and . . ."—the therapist says to use *and*, not *but*—"we're not having pancakes today. We have pancakes when there's extra time, and today is a school day." August is opinionated and spunky. That's what I tell myself on generous days. On hard days, I am afraid he is unkind. I'm afraid I've failed to teach him to respect me.

I add butter to the pan and use a cookie cutter to make a heart-shaped hole in the bread. "No, no, no, no, no!" August slams his hand on the granite of the counter, his voice reaching a desperate shrill. I add the bread to the pan. "Mommy!" he yells to get my attention. I crack the egg. "You're not listening to me!" I look up from my task and check the high chair, where Ace has grabbed a handful of Cheerios and is watching them slip from his fist and fall to the wood floor.

"August, I hear you," I say, still staring at Ace. "I already answered you. We can't have pancakes today." I know how this goes. He will get stuck on this expectation. He will believe he needs pancakes, and he won't let it go. He will cry until I give in or we arrive at school thirty minutes late. Either way, this won't get better. I grab some blueberries to place on Ace's tray. Then I flip the bread with its heart-shaped egg. It's 6:50.

"I need pancakes right now!" I ignore my oldest child at the counter. Fear bubbles in my throat. Will he scream? Will he refuse to put on his clothes? Will he take his cup and throw it? I look from August to Brooks, who has a cup of milk with a straw in it. Brooks sits still, lips on the straw in his cup. He twinkles his eyes at me when I catch his attention. He's waiting to see where this goes.

I hear Chris's steps on the stairs. My chest twists. Either he will help, or he and August will have a brawl of words. In both scenarios, Ace still won't have eaten breakfast.

"August!" Chris, wrapped in a towel, stomps into the kitchen. "Why do I hear you yelling at your mom?" I place the dinosaur egg in front of Brooks. August begins crying.

"You promised me we would have pancakes! You promised!" I turn to Chris, eyebrows raised, challenging him. He knows better than to make promises to this one who never forgets a pancake promised at bedtime.

"Aug, pancakes are on Saturday."

"No! You said tomorrow is special because it's the one-hundredth day of school, and you said we would celebrate, and today is tomorrow."

"It sounds like you thought 'celebrate' means pancakes."

"Of course it means pancakes."

I cut a fourth of an avocado into tiny cubes and walk to Ace's high chair. "Hey, baby," I say quietly, August's cries taking up all the energy in the room. Ace looks up at me, and I scoop a few avocado bites onto his tray. "I need you to eat some of this."

Fifteen minutes later, Chris has moved August off the stool and onto the floor. He's crying in Chris's toweled lap. It's 7:05. In the next ten minutes, my husband needs to ride his bike ten blocks to where the shuttle picks him up. From there he has an hour and a half commute to Silicon Valley. And in those same ten minutes, August and Brooks need to get dressed, brush their teeth, and find their backpacks. And Ace, who hasn't had any food yet, will have to be schlepped along. He is too small, losing weight, recently diagnosed with "failure to thrive." The dietician sat beside me two weeks ago and breezily explained how I could overcome this problem. I can add oil to his mashed-up avocado. Add butter to his potatoes. Smush more cream cheese into everything. "Just take your time with him," she said. My time? My time is spent like this.

August is crying in Chris's arms, and Chris looks at me. "I have to go," he mouths.

"Don't you dare," I mouth back.

"Augie, it's time for me to go," he says.

"No! No, Daddy. No, Daddy! Please don't leave me." Since toddlerhood, August has carried an inner intensity that, when compared to other children, feels different. He lives on high alert, attempting to control an uncontrollable world. His presence is big, whether he's delighted or afraid. So in moments of frustration and fear, he's an energy magnet. All of the gravity in the room pulls us straight to him. In a healthy frame of mind, August is tender, funny, and deeply creative. But when his expectations aren't met, he moves into fight or flight. At home, where he feels safe, his *fight* shows up louder than his *flight*.

Chris peels August's hands off his arm, and I look at my husband like a scared animal. "You got this, babe," he says as he hurries off to get dressed. I know he has to go. We have only one car, and I use it to cart the kids around. If he misses his shuttle, he'll be late for an important meeting with a client. But I still feel like I'm being fed to the wolves. August falls onto the floor and sobs.

* * *

When Jesus sits on a rock in the sunshine, calling out to his neighbors a poem of *makarioi*, listing all who flourish in the new world he is bringing—the dream of God—he gives no recommendations, no tips on how to earn God's blessing. And he doesn't list rewards. This is a description of the kind of people Jesus will gather around himself,[12] a kind of promise and consolation. The first half of each description of *makarioi* points to the community's experience of the world. The second half speaks to the community's future.[13] And Jesus is inviting his listeners to enter into the space between. You poor ones, he is saying, you *ptōchoi*, the kingdom of God belongs to you. You are the caretakers of the dream of God. This isn't a blessing that turns the poor rich. It's not sentimental either, not some squishy notion of sweetness to make everyone feel better about the fact that too many human beings live in conditions of hunger, neglect, and poverty. Jesus gives his pronouncements in a way that prioritizes the ones who have always been ignored. He is saying, "In the community of God, these are the ones we will center. Here, in this way of living, the poor and the poor in spirit will be prioritized." Jesus is establishing a vision of God that honors the ones who have lived their lives without honor. Because when we center the ones who have always been ignored, communities are healed.[14]

I have come from a religious culture that honors Christian celebrity, spiritual acumen, and the appearance of perfection. But that's not the story Jesus is telling on the hill. The community he is building offers relief from performance, from the relentless pursuit of being good enough. In Jesus's new vision of life, the ones who recognize their need for God are the ones who experience God's closeness.[15]

Maybe that's why I'm drawn to this passage, why I'm still drawn to Jesus. This is the kind of faith that makes sense in a world where the poor in spirit are still poor, even after they go home from hearing the preacher on the hill. A faith that doesn't pretend that a sentimental notion can make a baby gain weight or an anxious eight-year-old feel safe.

This is a blessing for empty people, for the marginalized, the miserable. In his poem, Jesus sets a new kind of faith story in motion: a countercultural invitation to a radical community in which the poor and the poor in spirit are invited into the place of honor. "God is especially there," with them.[16] Jesus uses present-tense language in this promise: the kingdom of heaven *is* theirs. Right now, in this world that divides us into the haves and the have-nots, God's dream is coming especially for the one groaning under the burden of poverty. "The kingdom of God belongs to them," most of our translations say. They are caretakers of the dream of God.

Ace spits out the avocado. Brooks finishes his dinosaur egg and hops down from the barstool. "Thanks, Mom!" He smiles, overcompensating for the rest of the scene.

"You're welcome, buddy," I say, forcing a smile.

Later, after I come home from taking the boys to school, I'll try to feed Ace again. I'll sit with him for an hour, slowly offering tiny spoonfuls of the avocado that will by then have turned brown. He will swallow some, but not enough. It never feels like enough. In two weeks, I'll take him back to the doctor, and he will weigh the same. I'll cry.

But for now, I put more Cheerios on his tray. "Brooksie," I say, "I'll come help you get dressed in a second."

I kneel down on the floor, where August is curled alongside Ace's Cheerios and chunks of avocado. I wrap my body around his. "Sh," I say. "You're okay."

In a former version of myself, this boy's anger was something I did my best to squelch with my own anger. "Don't you dare yell at me," I would hiss. "Don't you talk to me like that!"

Therapy has helped us both. My son's anxiety rages in him, and I cannot heal him with my own fear. It's still in my nature to want to yell back, and I often do. But it never fixes the pain in him. It only ignites his fire. And I've learned the hard way that his fire hurts him more than it does me.

"When I went to sleep last night, I told myself I was going to have pancakes." He hiccups. "Because it's a special day."

"Mommyyyyy!" Brooks calls from down the hall.

"I'll be there soon, honey!" I shout back. "It sounds like you're really disappointed," I say to August as I look at the clock: 7:15. *We're officially late.*

"You don't care! You don't care what I want," August says. Ace throws avocado in my hair.

"Aug, look at me." He lifts his splotchy face, his lips red and swollen. "I love you. And I always care what you want. *And . . .*" I mentally pat myself on the back for using the therapist's phrasing, "you need to get ready for school now. You can have a granola bar in the car."

I remind myself that being late isn't the worst thing that could happen. But my body tells me it is. This is the story I've been chasing my whole life: *Be perfect, Micha. Don't screw this up.* And lateness means I've failed. I feel a zipper across my chest tighten, each interlocking tooth clicking into place. My breath comes short and quick. *No,* I tell my body. *Slow down. Breathe.* August hiccups. "Max said his dad is richer than my dad. And he gets to watch *Predator* whenever he wants." Now we're getting to it. I take another long breath. He hiccups again.

"Max has some cool stuff," I manage to say calmly. "He has a Tesla."

"Yeah, 'cause his dad's rich. And his parents let him watch cool movies and you don't."

Another slow breath. "Families have different rules, right?"

He sits up and sucks in his own deep breaths, wiping his eyes. "Yep, and yours are dumb."

I wipe his wet cheeks with my thumb. I was a kid who never spoke to her parents with anger. I was polite, gentle. I worry endlessly about what August's anger says about him, about me. But if I can step outside of my own anxiety and let my chest zipper release a bit, I can better process the moment: August is afraid.

45

I'm overwhelmed. Ace is happy and hungry. Brooks is patiently humming a song down the hall. A frantic thought arises that Brooks, as the middle child, has begun to believe his value is found only in his ability to keep us smiling, to make us okay. All around me I see the breakdown of health and wholeness I wanted for all of us.

"August, you need to stand up and go get your clothes on. It's time for school."

My chest zipper loosens a bit more when he stands and walks to the bathroom. I find Brooks playing with LEGOs in his underwear in his bedroom. It will take us ten minutes to drive to school, which begins ten minutes from now. No amount of rushing will get us there on time. I give myself permission to slow down. I grab a sweatshirt and shorts from the drawer. "Did you go pee this morning, Brooksie?" He smiles at me like he has a secret.

"Yes," he says while he shakes his head no.

"Brooksie, go to the bathroom," I say. He giggles and runs off. August is brushing his teeth. He's breathing normally now.

"Mama, I do want a Tesla, though," he says, mouth full of blue foam.

"I know you do, babe," I say, walking back into the kitchen, where I grab a washcloth from the kitchen sink, wet it, squeeze it out, and carry it to the lone baby still sitting, empty bellied, in his high chair. *I am a caretaker of the dream of God.*

"We'll try again later," I say to Ace. He kicks his baby legs. "Buddy," I say, unlatching the tray and his seat belt, "you have to eat. I need you to eat." I pick up his body, his low muscle tone snuggle makes him feel like a sack of flour pressing into my chest and belly. He wraps his arms around my neck, and I feel his hand brush my skin there.

"Mom! I need help!" Brooks yells.

Their needs are relentless, and I'm not sure it's going to get easier. We're late again. My baby is shrinking. I don't know what I believe. I feel my own poverty, which I suppose makes me uniquely qualified for this particular job: "You are a caretaker of the dream of God," I whisper to myself, shoving backpacks onto their hungry, heartbroken, always-striving bodies. I open the door to the garage.

I'm invited to be a caretaker. And maybe they're the dream.

2

For the Ones Who Grieve

Makarioi are the ones who grieve. They will be invited to a divine banquet.

DECEMBER 2016 (ACE, TWENTY MONTHS OLD)
SAN FRANCISCO

Brooks kneels beside his Magna-Tiles, ignoring my requests that he open his drawer and find his pajamas. He selects a green plastic square to click into place. I hold Ace steady on the navy shag carpet of the room the three boys share, his wiggling an annoyance as I attempt to get a new diaper into place. August hangs at an angle by his right hand from the bunk bed, his right foot on the bottom bunk, like a circus performer pausing mid-act to acknowledge the crowd. He is pumped. "Colin says his friend has a first edition Charizard card and it's worth a thousand dollars!" I nod my head, no desire to hear about Pikachu or Charizard or the world of Pokémon trading cards August spends every recess navigating. I'm trying—and failing—to listen, wishing I'd chosen the chore of dishes tonight and let Chris wrangle this collection of boy energy into bed.

"Brooksie, pajamas on, buddy," I say as Ace wiggles out of my hands and crawls, right knee on the floor, left foot propelling him forward—his signature move these days—toward Brooks's mess of tiles. Then he changes course. He squats and turns his head to catch my eye. He smiles. Earlier in the afternoon, he discovered the possibilities of a sumo squat, and I can tell he has plans to stand up, just as soon as his legs, slowed down by low muscle tone, stop wobbling like Jell-O. He just needs to figure out how to make that happen. He moves from hands and knees to bear crawl, feet pressing into the carpet, then pushes off, his chest lifting to vertical, legs vibrating for a beat. Then he drops to his butt, his diaper cushioning the smash of his body into the carpet, and giggles.

August stops his one-way discussion of Pokémon. "Daddy!" he calls toward the kitchen, a short hallway from the boys' room. "Acey's trying to stand!" Before Ace even goes for a third attempt, we've all stopped our tasks and semicircled around the haphazardly diapered toddler, who repeats his attempts at standing again and again. All fours to downward dog, then a squat as he lifts his hands from the ground to the air, shouting, "Aah!" and crashing hard. We can't stop watching and giggling, and Ace won't stop trying, his mouth wide open, his eyes shining at us. We take to shouting "Aah!" with him too. It feels necessary, as if our joining him in his language will hold him, steady his chest toward the sky.

As he approaches age two, Ace mostly makes that "aah" sound all the time, with a few other consonants like "dah" and sometimes "bah." It's a sign of the struggle with language and speech that will be part of his ongoing story. At this point in his life, he approximates some words like "Dada" and "Ada" (for August) but never makes it to the "mah" sound required for "Mama." And though a few times I think I hear him call Brooks "See" for "Brooksie," his brother's name will eventually be lost inside him, in the cavernous language gorge Ace will struggle to excavate for years to come. But at this point, we hear words in his sounds, wobbling like his legs toward what we hope will be a future sturdiness.

For twenty minutes, Ace squats and falls. We cheer and laugh. I check the clock, aware of how far past bedtime we've already inched. Just as I'm about to shut the whole thing down and force all the little boy bodies into beds, Ace shouts, "Aah!" lifts his chest, and balances his torso over his two uncertain feet. Our cheers rise up pure and loud. "One, two, three!" And then he's on the ground, smile wide, big eyes moving back and forth to all of us with delight.

I'm laughing when I turn to see August beside me wiping a big, hot tear, confused by his own emotional state. I recognize the heavy joy on his face. I know this feeling. Eight and a half years earlier, when August crashed his way into the world and landed in my arms, I was cosmically altered by the sight of my newborn's face—he was *real*, more real than almost anything I'd set my eyes on. My joy felt seismic as I cradled his never-yet-touched body while the lower half of me quivered under the force of post-birth trauma—blood, placenta, stitches, the clean-up crew. In the dangerous and shimmering reality of the moment, holding his miracle life, I was made of laughter and tears—all my love and fear, pain and relief stirred into one another, effervescent, bubbling out of me. Everything at once.

Now, August is beside me on the shag carpet, his third-grade body discovering the same devastating power, how love and sadness need each other, how they live together.

I meet his eyes and feel my tears too.

He scoots toward me and drapes his arms and head across my legs, his body shaking while he cries. "I know, buddy," I say. I know. Oblivious to August, Ace continues his balancing act, pushing himself up, wobbling, then holding his standing posture for a breath. Chris and Brooks cheer.

"Why am I crying, Mom?" August asks, lifting his shoulders so he can look up from the pillow of my lap. Being Ace's mom has taught me to see my grief and my deep love for my baby as a braid woven through my chest, pulled tight. I don't have to know where the love ends and the sorrow begins, only that they wrap around each other. But how do I explain this to his older brother, that the love I felt when I first saw Ace was not diminished by the sorrow I carried? That love is never diminished by pain, that love and suffering have been cohabiting companions as long as love has existed on this earth?

"I think it's probably because you love him so much," I say as I brush aside the blond skater swoop he's insisted on growing. It's wet enough from his tears to stay in place. I stare in his eyes, like I did that early summer night when he arrived in my world, with all the love I can muster, all the joy and compassion I have room to hold in my center. He knows that most of Ace's peers learned to stand twelve months ago. In a few months, I'll bring home the metal, hospital-grade toddler walker Ace will use to take his first tentative steps. His milestones will be different all the way through his life, and somehow in this moment, August feels the sadness of that, right beside his joy. He lets go of me and sits up, wiping his face on his sleeve.

Ace yells, "Aah!" then falls on his butt and claps his hands.

DECEMBER 2014
SAN FRANCISCO

In the weeks that follow the geneticist's call informing me that the baby I carry will be born with Down syndrome, I wake each morning with a tightness in my lungs, as if overnight my anxiety built a lattice of fear, right where my air ought to flow. Down syndrome, the muted glow of winter sunshine says to me through the window. Down syndrome, the birds chirp when I step outside. Down syndrome, the fog whispers as it rises from the Pacific and rushes toward my house every afternoon. My research tells me all I have to be afraid of: the 50 percent chance of a heart defect, the high percentage of blood cancers, the low muscle tone, the possible hearing loss or gastrointestinal problems, the number of babies with Down syndrome born too early, unable to latch on to the breast or process food correctly so they grow at a healthy pace.

And every morning I find the same task waiting for me. I bring one hand to my fear-woven chest and the other hand to my belly, where beneath my skin and ever-expanding fleshy uterus, the baby I carry is becoming himself. I breathe. Then I open my hands to release the imaginary child, the one who didn't have Down syndrome, the one I know will never be.

Grief has a way of transforming our interior soil, digging itself deep in the places most vulnerable, most tender inside us. It always hurts, always cuts us open. And in the dream God dreams, in the community Jesus is creating on the hill outside Capernaum, grief is never ignored or glossed over. Jesus never stands in front of his listeners and denies their pain. He has no trite sentimentalities to share: no "everything happens for a reason," no "sometimes God closes a door and opens a window." I imagine Jesus holding the depth of the really real of this world: Sometimes children die of starvation, and earthquakes collapse buildings. Sometimes the plane crashes. Sometimes the cancer returns. So when he blesses, when he speaks *makarioi* to the ones on the hill who mourn, he promises something better than a nice platitude.

"*Makarioi* are the ones who grieve," Jesus says, his eyes on a crowd of those who have every reason to mourn, living as they do in a world where a quarter of all children die in their first year of life and around half of all children are lost before they reach puberty.[1] Life is fragile, dangerous, with infectious diseases, unstable economic structures, and in the case of the crowd around Jesus, an oppressive empire that controls their every day. It has always been excruciating to be human, but in ancient Palestine, ruled by the powers of Rome, grief is a constant companion.

On the hill, at the beginning of his sermon, Jesus offers a vision of grief not as a part of life to avoid or move past but as a path toward the selves God has made us to be. A way toward flourishing.[2] The word most often translated in Matthew 5:4 as "mourn" is *pentheō*, a word that points to intimate, acute, devastating sorrow.[3] We don't have many descriptive words for that kind of sorrow. In English, we mostly use metaphors, images of hearts cracked open that can't be sealed back together. Or waves that knock us backward and hold us under water.

And, of course, what we mean by these metaphors is that the place we stored our joy, our hope of a certain kind of future, has been invaded without our permission. Joy will never feel safe there again. What we mean is that once we loved with a lightness, an ease, and now we know that the lightness was never actually there to begin with. It was a trick, and it can always be stolen again.

The baby I had believed I was carrying—the one I imagined before my twenty-week ultrasound, the one whose grainy image in the sonogram machine didn't show a calcium deposit in the heart—is gone. That baby never actually existed. They call this disenfranchised grief, grief that has no face, no missing person. It's grief over an idea. I mourn the alternate story. And I don't know how to name my sorrow as I move from the diagnosis into the last twenty weeks of my pregnancy.

I learn to pray four words again and again. "I receive my child," I say to the sunshine, to the birds, to the coming fog. I receive him, and I receive this story, the real one. However it may go.

Years later, I'll learn that the egg with the trisomy 21 genetic anomaly was always inside me. Down syndrome is always passed from the mother. So I carried the particular egg that formed Ace from the moment all the eggs formed in my ovaries. I'll research this fact later: one million eggs already inside a girl at birth, three hundred thousand by puberty, only three to four hundred that will ovulate in a woman's lifetime. That this egg survived will become a wonder to me. "Women's bodies become less discriminating over time," a friend, another mom of a child with Down syndrome, will later tell me. "Younger bodies are more likely to reject eggs with genetic variations. But older bodies? They're more hospitable." *Thank you for your hospitality*, I'll think, my hand on my low belly where my uterus has worked so hard for me all these years, egg after egg. Such a wonder that this egg—the egg that became Ace—is the one we culled.

● ● ●

When we interpret the blessings of Jesus in the Beatitudes as a new way of living in the world, a way in which our suffering is not just part of true human flourishing but a path toward it, we find an invitation. We are invited not to rejoice in our grief and loss in this life but to transform our thinking around what it means to have a full, thriving life in the midst of our suffering. Jesus invites his listeners to consider that the darkest pain of their lives has always been an invitation to know God, an invitation into a community in which we orient ourselves toward the dream of God, not denying our pain but allowing it to be the sharp edge that, like the plowshare prepares the soil, makes space in us for new, transformative life.[4]

The blessing Jesus offers on the hill is "they will be comforted." The word is *parakaleō*, which means both the experience of consolation and an invitation to a banquet[5]—dichotomies that perhaps aren't that far from each other. It's just that most of us don't want to be invited to the banquet of grief.

During the foggy days of December, after the prenatal diagnosis, the world around me is lit by twinkle lights and draped in evergreen, so I think about Mary, the mother of Jesus, and whether she received comfort (or a banquet) in her prenatal grief. In the Message version of the gospel of Luke, where we find her famous song of liberation in the first chapter, she doesn't seem sad at all. Still, Luke doesn't tell us everything, so I like to assume she mourned her former ordinary and safe existence and the improbable pregnancy she couldn't have planned for. "[God's] mercy flows in wave after wave on those who are in awe before him," she sang. *Wave after wave.*

Each morning I practice releasing my imaginary child and embracing my real child. I imagine his future, this boy I love who will live with intellectual disability. And I imagine Mary's sacred mercy splashing onto her over and over. Maybe, I think, she understood what all of us who learn to swim in the ocean must discover the hard way: when the waves come, we dive under them. Either that, or we find ourselves held under, upside down, face against the sandbar. Those waves can appear at first as loss. But eventually, suffering can transform itself into power and beauty. Maybe it depends on which way we encounter the waves of grief, as power we can't overcome or as mercy washing us clean.

*　*　*

Two days after my prenatal diagnosis, I call my brother Brooks, after whom my middle son is named. I stand among a pile of laundry in the family room, forcing myself to fold clothes and say the words out loud on the phone: Down syndrome. Our baby will have Down syndrome. My voice wavers; Brooks's voice cracks on the other side. I fold August's Batman T-shirt. "How did Mom take it?" he asks, knowing I'd already mustered the courage for that phone call.

My mom has worked in the public school system as an early intervention teacher for hard-of-hearing and deaf students for forty years. And in addition to serving the deaf community during her years of teaching, she's taught and loved children with physical and intellectual disabilities. "She cried," I say, "then told me it was going to be wonderful."

"Well," Brooks says, "I mean, all her dreams are finally coming true."

I laugh, my hands dropping the stack of clean little-boy clothes. I laugh until I'm kneeling on the carpet wiping my eyes. I laugh because this is a kind of brutal mercy, my mother's love for children with Down syndrome, whom she has taught and adored in her life as a teacher. Mercy, to have one last grandchild, and for that youngest to be the child she had spent her career learning to honor above all the rest. Mercy, because to know the beauty of a child with a disability is always, simultaneously, to know the ache. I kneel in the pile of clothes, my brother laughing along with me through the screen of my phone, sharing the truth and joy of this: I will never be alone in my story, my son's story. And even this laughter is preparation for the miracle of Ace's birth.

Pain and loss will come for all of us. Grief is a required ritual of human existence, a mysterious concoction of vulnerability and love, with the power to gut us from chest to belly. Maybe Mary knew that the waves of mercy and the waves of grief are often one and the same for those brave enough to hold their breath and swim through.

I receive my child, Lord, I pray eight weeks later, gazing at my body in the bathroom mirror. I wear a loose, light-blue hospital gown. Chris sits on the other side of the door in a dark room, where the lights are dimmed and the fetal echocardiogram technician waits for me. Soon I'll pull the sheet up to the base of my belly and lift my hospital gown, exposing my middle to gel and sticky patches, the hands of strangers connecting my body to wires to decipher the mysteries of our baby. *I receive my child,* I pray. I open the door to the room, offering myself to the table and its instruments. During the next thirty minutes, every movement of the fetus on the screen will represent an unknown-to-me possible fear. Will he come out of me and into the air with a heart that works? Will his blood pump slow and languish in his body? Will he pale and shiver in the world, rushed by hands other than mine into a warmed glass cage, forced to spend his first days separated from me? I love him. And I'm terrified of him.

I receive my child.

His heart works, the technician assures us. Chris and I laugh and cry a little. One nightmare removed from the list. And still each morning I wake to a tide inside me—joy and fear—rising, falling. I'm filled with the same body I mourn, so I breathe myself out of bed.

DECEMBER 2016
SAN FRANCISCO

When Ace stands for the first time, August cries, not because
he understands the science of Ace's chromosomes or why Ace
has low muscle tone or the reality that he has worked twice as
hard as a typical child to build his strength. August cries because
he's lived his brother's first twenty months beside him. He has
sat in waiting rooms through countless doctors' appointments,
has welcomed the physical, occupational, and speech therapists
who crowd into our living room each week to roll Ace on top of
an exercise ball, or massage his arms, or play with toy animals
and sing.

August knows that his own body learned to stand simply because he progressed naturally toward that moment, because his
legs and ankles and feet cooperated with his body's development.
And he knows that Ace's body requires so much more than age-
appropriate natural progress. Even as a child, August is being
formed by the struggle of watching someone he loves work harder
than everyone else and still end up the last in line. He's beginning
to feel the weight of how this world operates. He is—I hope—
learning to ache for justice.

I run my hand through August's blond waves. We humans cannot run long from grief. The blessing Jesus offers the ones who
mourn is a blessing for the ones who love. Perhaps Jesus's mother
taught him that story, how loving anyone is an invitation to mercy,
which comes to us in wave after suffocating wave. I wonder if
Mary sat with her son like this, on the floor of a simple room, his
body spread across her legs, her fingers tucking his hair behind
his ear. His body, mind, and soul the other side of a pregnancy
that had sometimes left her terrified and resentful. Perhaps Jesus
knew what it was to come from a pregnancy first grieved, then

transformed into joy. How a child—like magic—becomes a person, not just an idea.

Perhaps he remembered this when he gave his blessing for the grieving ones. As the poet sang, "Those who go out weeping, bearing the seed for sowing, shall come home with shouts of joy, carrying their sheaves."[6] Jesus knew that always within grief there is a seed of mercy. He promised to people who knew everything there was to know about grief that even as they weep, they carry seed to the field. And maybe the banquet, the feast that will come, lies on the other side of that planted seed.

The invitation to the banquet of grief throws open the doors of suffering to reveal the kind of flourishing known only to those who have gone out with weeping and stepped back through with shouts of joy. These tears August cries are my first recognition that he has walked through those doors too.

"Okay, people," I say, my hand on August's head, my gaze turning to Chris, who moves from his seat to his knees to tackle Ace, mid-squat, into a hug. "To bed." Brooks jumps onto Chris's back while Ace squeals, his body bare except for his diaper. A body just like mine: two arms, two legs, round belly. A face that looks so perfectly like his brothers' faces—the same nose, blue eyes, eyebrows straight from my grandmother's face—that sometimes I forget to see the facial features common to Down syndrome at all.

August stands and leaps into the pile. Chris tickles Ace's ribs, Brooks and August drape over their dad's legs and shoulders. They are loud as a banquet, all shouts of joy.

3

For the Ones Who Release Their Power

Makarioi are the powerless ones and the ones who re-lease their power. They will recognize that the entire earth has always been theirs.

I step into Ace's second-grade classroom on a rainy East Coast fall day. It's pajama day, and the kids sitting on the carpet are wearing a hodgepodge of *Star Wars*, *Frozen*, and polka-dot two-piece out-fits. Ace has been placed in a classroom with two teachers, one a general education teacher, the other a special education teacher. And he has a one-on-one aide. While he's not the only kid in the room with a disability, he is the only one who is nonspeaking and the only child still learning to properly control a crayon in a class that has moved on to reading two-syllable words.

Ace is the size of a four-year-old, wearing toddler-size Yoda pajamas that make him look like a little sibling among his peers. They are talking to one another, coloring, or looking at the books in the corner. Ace has found a lid from a container in the play area to spin on a table. He loves making things spin. When he hears my voice in his classroom, he looks up and smiles, obviously happy about my arrival, something I talked to him about ahead of time. He even touches my face with his hand when I squat down to say hello. But he goes quickly back to spinning the lid, ignoring the kids in the classroom as much as he's ignoring me.

Chris and I have worked hard to get to this point. Inclusive education is a challenge for schools and families, but studies have consistently proven that children with intellectual disabilities who are welcomed into a greater school community and learn alongside their typically developing peers grow into adults with more confidence, independence, and life skills.[1] Most of the time, a child with a disability needs to be functioning at a level close enough to their typical peers to make their presence in the classroom feel doable for the school. The kids labeled "higher functioning" are more likely to be placed in inclusive environments, while the kids with more challenges stay in segregated classrooms, because the distractions and the gaps in what the students are learning can feel too difficult for educational systems to overcome.

This seems normal in our culture. Of course, it's difficult for a teacher to instruct a classroom of students at one particular level of development while also teaching a child at a completely different and unique level of development. But inclusion is a concept that can't demand prerequisites. People are either included or they're not. When inclusive practices are based on merit, the entire system of generosity and openness is removed.

True inclusion can't require a skill set or ability to fit a mold. The work of inclusion is the work of welcome: who you are is who we want. This is a tricky proposition for the classroom, where merit and like-mindedness often feel necessary for a functioning learning environment. But every once in a while, the students and the teacher catch a vision for something else, for a learning community in which everyone doesn't have to be the same.

I gather the group to sit in a circle on the floor and begin a conversation about differences. I have a paper box in my hand with questions on it: What is something you like about the person next to you? What makes you special? We throw the box and answer questions that I'm keenly aware Ace can't yet answer for himself. His aide sits beside him with his iPad communication device, what we call his "talker," in case he decides to make the kind of simple statement he makes from time to time by pressing its images: "I want to read" or "Stop" or "I want mango." So far, he hasn't used his device to tell me how he feels, and he won't be answering my question, What makes you special? He doesn't stay crisscross applesauce for long and instead comes over to my seat in front of his classmates and lays his head on my lap for a moment.

"What ways are all of us the same?" Ace sits back up to lean against my shoulder. Someone says something about hair or having eyes or arms. Then Ace stands up and runs to the other side of the circle making his classic sound: "Aah!"

"What ways are we different?"

There are moments when I see my son and catch my breath, taken by the beauty of how he moves and exists in his body so differently from the ways I inhabit mine. There are also moments when I am awed all over again that he exists and moments when I feel the sting of his first diagnosis. I have spoken and written a thousand words in hopes that his world will transform to hold his humanity, his particular glory. And still I find life ruthlessly capable of moving on without him. In this room, his responses, his sounds don't mimic those of his peers at all. He is only himself. I hold the grief of his originality in the same breath as I praise it.

"I want you to know that it's really special to our family that you are Ace's classmates. Ace really loves being with you and getting to be part of room 7, even if he doesn't always sit as still as some of you do. Even if he doesn't raise his hand to answer the questions. What kinds of things does Ace do to show that he's participating in your classroom?"

A little boy named Henry raises his hand. "He says, 'Aah.'"

"Yep," I say. "He says that a lot, doesn't he? What else?"

Amelia, who gave Ace a handmade cut-out note last week where she had scribbled, "You are a good friend," raises her hand. "Ace gives high fives," she says.

"I wonder if when Ace is giving high fives, he's trying to say more than just hi. Maybe he wants to say, 'I like you.' Or maybe he wants to say, 'I'm glad you're my friend.'" Amelia nods her head. She's obviously given this a lot of thought.

"Have you ever had a time when you really wanted to say something but it was hard to get it out? Maybe you were nervous or scared. Or maybe you felt like everyone was being really loud around you and you didn't think anyone could hear you." Five kids wave their hands, hoping to tell their stories. I keep going. "Why do you think it might be hard for Ace to talk?"

The kids have a lot of answers. And most of them are correct. I find that most of the time, children understand Ace much more than adults do. They answer my questions, and Ace eventually sits still. I read a book about two girls putting on a play in a park. Every child who comes to join their play comes with his or her own particular limitation: speech, sight, physical ability. And every time they ask to join, the sisters reply, "Exactly who you are is exactly who we pick!"[2]

Before I leave the room, I lean down close to Ace's face to catch his eyes, as eye contact is a challenge for him. "I like your class," I whisper in his ear, thinking of the note Amelia made that hangs on our refrigerator. "You are a good friend."

JULY 2022
NORTHERN MINNESOTA

It's 7:00 a.m., and I'm alone, a guest in the woods outside a college campus where I'm staying for a writing retreat. I've coated myself with bug spray and am wearing a John Deere trucker hat that doesn't belong to me because last time I hiked this path two days ago, some wildly big bugs tried to build homes in my hair.

In the past few months, I have become convinced that the Beatitudes are both a language and a way of being that explain something Ace has already taught me, that the "good life"—the life with God—is found precisely in the place where no one else is looking.[3] As Ace has grown, I've begun to recognize that his small way of being and his slow way of doing are transforming me toward smallness, toward slowness. In a world where we use size and speed—efficiency—to prove our importance, our productivity can become our "personal salvation project."[4] We show the world that we are worthy of being alive by doing our jobs, raising our kids, impressing the right people, and we consider this normal. But the more I've known my son, the more I've seen Jesus's words with new clarity. In this poem, his list of *makarioi*, Jesus is inviting his listeners to a transformative kind of antiefficiency. The ones whom God is especially with, the ones who are living whole and thriving lives, are the ones who are small, the ones who are becoming smaller. The good life just might exist in the places I would never have known to look.

While I hike, I try to memorize lines from a poem by Rainer Maria Rilke:

> Quiet friend who has come so far . . .
> let this darkness be a bell tower
> and you the bell. As you ring
> what batters you becomes your strength.[5]

I wonder about what batters me, what batters Ace. He's lived his life as the last in line. But there's also a kind of phenomenon that follows Ace around. People who experience his presence can find themselves quieted, calmed, even delighted. This often comes as a surprise. Ace isn't what people expect he'll be. He needs more help, but he isn't needy. He struggles to engage socially, but he is deeply in tune emotionally. There is a lightness in his presence, a release from the tyranny of hustle culture. The energy around him is soft, not because he's angelic or perfect but because he doesn't demand time or explanation from the people who move in and out of his orbit. His is a presence of rest. He has all the time in the world.

The rules of our society weren't written for him. Every year he is further and further behind in the expectations of our educational system. He is too small for the sports teams his peers play on. When he is grown, the job offerings available for his skill set will most likely not be enough to support him financially. He probably won't fit expectations of what makes a person able to contribute to the economy, support his community, or even offer his friends or family the emotional or physical care most of us expect from the loved ones in our lives. Even so, I wonder if Ace is the free one, unable to meet our cultural expectations of what makes a good life. And he lives as a nondemanding presence for the rest of us, reminding us that we don't have to meet those expectations either.

Maybe that's what Jesus is spelling out for us: *makarioi* are the ones who have been released from the pressure to win. What if the child least likely to be told "exactly who you are is exactly who we pick" is the one who holds the secret to the whole game?

The promise for the meek might be why I came to the Beatitudes in the first place, hoping that I might build for Ace a robust vision of his place in the dream of God, that Jesus's words might confirm my suspicion that, despite Ace being the last to speak, the last to use a crayon, and the one spinning a lid alone in the classroom, he is the first in line in this dream. He is the one for whom love, the most important human experience, comes easy. Or as Jesus says to the crowd gathered on the hill, flourishing are the ones who release their power, because they "inherit the world."[6] I need to understand what it means to inherit the world, because I want Ace, my powerless child, to have the honor of inheriting everything he can't earn himself, everything the world says doesn't belong to him.

On the trail, I recite Rilke's poem over and over to the sound of my feet scraping the dirt, *shoosh, shoosh, shoosh*. I speak it to the squirrel that shakes the bush as I approach: "Move back and forth into the change."[7]

I see what I think is a redheaded woodpecker—with its black-and-white-lined body—dash across the water. While I'm away, Ace is back at home, taking the bus each morning to summer school. "Extended school year," they call it, where he works with his therapists, attempts to establish his communication skills using his talker. At home it's how he asks Chris to play with him on the trampoline. "I want to jump on the trampoline," the device's childlike robot voice says. Chris uses Ace's finger to push the next button that appears. "People," the screen says, and on the next screen are pictures of the four of us: Mom, Dad, August, Brooks. Ace touches a face. "I want to jump on the trampoline with Dad."

Flourishing are the ones who release their power. The poem I've been reciting, this notion of moving back and forth into the change of our lives, this sense that what batters us becomes our strength, may point somehow to what meekness means. When our power is contained, whether through life circumstances or through our own choice to release our power, we will always be battered. But it's the battering that shapes our lives; it's the battering that gives the bell its music.

Jesus's blessing of meekness often gets lost in translation, mostly because nobody uses the word *meek* anymore. I'm pretty sure most of us don't even know what it means. I always thought of meekness as interchangeable with weakness. But meekness is more akin to humility. It's defined in all sorts of variations: gentleness, powerlessness, nonviolence. And the more I explore the idea, the more I wonder if meekness actually has more to do with me than with my son. Maybe meekness is for those of us who know how to win in this world, those of us who have always, only known the privilege of acceptance and comfort. Maybe meekness is an invitation to move back and forth into the change around us, to allow ourselves to be contained by it. Maybe meekness is a new way of being human.

Though meekness can certainly be defined as the lack of strength, there's also a kind of meekness we can choose for ourselves: meekness as a spiritual practice. It's having access to power but choosing not to wield it for oneself. It's holding back our control, our comfort, our voice, in order to give that privilege to another. It's the advocate giving testimony on behalf of the one who doesn't speak the language of those in authority, the one who doesn't have time or energy to push for justice on their own behalf, or the one whose voice has been deemed by those in places of influence as unworthy of being heard. It's a person in a position of power who thinks creatively enough to notice where and how that power can be shared. The word we translate as "meek" comes from the Greek word *praus*. It refers to a wild animal that has been tamed, often a horse broken in, trained, and taken into war.[8] Meekness is an invitation to be tamed, to lay our power down, to move toward gentleness and nonviolence, especially when other options are available to us.[9] Meekness requires releasing our hold and control. It asks us to join the powerless in the back of the line. *Move back and forth into the change.*

There is a narrow and particular stream that holds the world's version of happiness: be beautiful, be healthy, be pleasant, be successful, the stream demands. Those of us who can float down that stream without complaining or noticing who is missing from the water are rewarded with value. "You are good!" our systems say to some. "You are a burden," our systems say to others. Our schools and organizations, programs and churches, love those of us who show up in ways that make people comfortable. Power is easy. It's pleasant. But difference? Meekness? It's dangerous. Not toilet-trained and seven years old? Making weird noises while you play? Flapping your hands when you're supposed to sit still and not distract others? "We don't know what to do with you," the stream says.

To reject this way of evaluating human worth is to release our power and our comfort. It's the practice of meekness: turning our bodies around midstream and moving against the current that the world's "approved ones" float down. Those who go upstream—by choice or circumstance—find themselves exhausted, overwhelmed by pressure on all sides. And sometimes it feels like there is no end to the journey. Where is the source of this stream? And what could it ever mean to transform it? Sometimes in the process we come across another human coming downstream, propelled along by the systems that allow their ease and success. The good-hearted ones call out as they pass us: "I really admire how you're swimming up this stream! What a difficult thing to do!" It's the equivalent of the "your kid with Down syndrome is an angel" meme that Boomers send moms like me on Facebook.

Those with intellectual or physical disabilities are hardly the only ones forced to push against systems that aren't built for them. In fact, as a straight, cis, white, economically stable woman, I needed to have a child with disabilities to see the cultural current for what it actually is: a complicated social structure of norms that keep many—the disabled but also Black people, Indigenous people, People of Color, LGBTQ+ folks, and those living with generational poverty—from the community, care, and opportunity offered to those deemed acceptable enough. Our social structures allow a privileged few to float downstream, blissfully unaware of how the river favors only the ones the world has deemed worthy.

The trail I'm hiking opens to a lake full of the greenest summer lily pads, the kind Monet would have painted had he made his way to Minnesota for a summer writing retreat. I stop and stare at the buds that grow out of the water, plants waiting to burst open. I'll be gone before they bloom. Across the water a bird I can't see calls out. I pull a bug from the part of my hair the trucker hat isn't covering.

Jesus doesn't just offer a nice blessing for the weak. He invites all of us, especially those of us who have spent our lives floating down the stream, to choose powerlessness so that we can join the ones who have been struggling against the current all their lives. Jesus tells his followers that there is a kind of flourishing found in allowing what batters us to become our strength. For those of us with cultural currency, those of us who have naturally, by luck, birth, and family history, found ourselves in the front of the line, these particular *makarioi* invite us to find our footing and turn our bodies around.

Makarioi are those who push against the cultural current that denies value to so many. Wise, flourishing, and becoming whole are we who learn to live utterly outside the rules of the stream, letting go of our ease so we can learn a new way of living: God's dream for the world. We join the ones who already have the most value in the currency of the really real.

I cross a flat bridge beside the lily pads and catch a glimpse of that bird I heard in the distance: a crane. I say the lines again: "Quiet friend who has come so far . . . / let this darkness be a bell tower / and you the bell. As you ring / what batters you becomes your strength."

I consider how loving Ace has contained me, how what looks like suffering has become my own flourishing: the darkness of the prenatal echocardiogram, the tears I've cried over his tiny body and its slow-motion growth. I think of each time I've released him into the hands of surgeons, how impossible it is to find a babysitter who will help a seven-year-old who isn't toilet-trained. I think of how kids stare at the park and the relentless calling I feel as Ace's mom to walk up to the staring child, smile, and introduce my son: "Ace doesn't talk very much," I say. "But he loves to play!"

I imagine myself as the wall of that bell, the clapper's tongue battering its darkness into me—my failures, my exhaustion, my fears—creating the beautiful tone I was intended to sing. What batters us becomes our strength, Rilke says. In fact, what batters us makes the music in which we find our purpose. Meekness becomes the work of living within our particular bell tower, letting ourselves be struck over and over by the challenges we face in our lives. And maybe that's what it means to become whole: to release our striving, to release our power, and allow ourselves to live as *praus*—wild ones, tamed for the sake of the other.

FEBRUARY 2023
NEW JERSEY

It's Valentine's Day, and Ace painstakingly writes a classmate's name on every valentine card we place in front of him. It takes three different sits and lots of dried mango bribery to get through all sixteen of them. Hand over hand, both Chris and I help Ace hold his marker while we control his movements, scratching out their names, and finally let him have control when he gets to the *e* on his name. Then he scratches marks all over the card.

At school, when he arrives, his friend Gabriela meets his bus. She and Amelia take turns. Ace loves being met by friends instead of his one-on-one aide. Gabi takes Ace's hand. He's a head shorter than her, and his backpack, filled to the brim with valentine cards, looks like it'll tip him over at any moment. She doesn't expect any words from Ace. She's learned throughout the school year that Ace won't say hi to her, though he will give her a high five, which he's gotten better and better at doing. They walk slowly into school together, letting the other kids their age run ahead. Ace can run, but not with a backpack and coat on. And he's content holding a friend's hand, making his way slowly each morning to room 7.

Later, after he and Gabi have hung up their backpacks and coats, after he's followed his friends to their spots on the carpet for circle time, Ace gets the chance to pass out his valentines. One at a time, his aide, Tawnya, reads the names he's written on the cards in his bag. One by one, she directs him to each child's spot in the circle, reminding him to look in their eyes. One by one, they take the cards he worked so hard to scratch his marker along. They give him valentines in return.

When he gets home, he's not all that interested in pulling out each valentine he's received, so I open them, showcasing and overly narrating his stash: "Look, a puppy eraser! Look, a sticker! Hey, Henry gave you a popper!" He ignores me. He wants to spin the plastic pool ring his grandma gave him in the valentine package she sent in the mail. So I let him stim, a necessary and beautiful part of how he lives in the world—flapping his hands, spinning circular toys, making "aah" sounds. All of these are ways his autistic body regulates itself in an overwhelming world.

I wait a bit before I settle in beside him on the carpet of the foyer. I catch his eyes. "Today was Valentine's Day!" I say. He smiles at me. "Did you have fun?"

He makes a sound, "Hmm," which his speech therapist has taught me to acknowledge as his answer to me. The more I supply a response as if he's answered me, the more likely he will begin to do this naturally.

"You did! You had fun!"

He spins the ring again. "I bet you gave a valentine to all your friends." And I start to list them, knowing this will get him going: "Gabi and Amelia, Enzo and Henry, and Aubrey." He's smiling now, letting the ring stop moving against his palm. He looks up at me and gives me a wide grin. "Oh, you did give them your

73

valentines! I hope they noticed that you wrote all their names yourself." Still smiling, he moves his eyes back to his ring and spins.

I struggle between pushing Ace to grow and my knowledge that he doesn't have to grow or change in order to be good. I don't need him to talk to earn his place as my beloved. I don't need him to read and write to be worthy of his humanity. I don't need him to call my name in order to call him my son. But language is power, and Ace appears to the world as powerless. So I continue to show up with him at therapy appointments, to practice our sounds and songs in the spaces between the chaos of daily life and our moments of play. And still, he can't tell me where he hurts with spoken words. He can't tell me how he feels. Last week, after two days of a high fever, when he refused to use signs or his talker or any of our communication cards to tell me what hurt, he finally lifted his hands to his chest and fake coughed. I sat beside him and put my hand over his.

"It really hurts right there," I said. He was diagnosed with pneumonia.

How do you thrive in a world where you can't communicate, where words fail you? How do you flourish when you can't tell your mom where it hurts?

When Jesus looks into the eyes of the mistreated working-class folks on the hillside and calls them whole in their meekness, I wonder how he makes sense of the vulnerability required of the meek. Ace's powerlessness rests in his inability to say what he needs, to tell us what he loves, to invite the full expression of relationship into his life. He is utterly dependent on the Gabis and Amelias of his life to take his hand and guide him. I long for him to be released from that dependence, to be able to hold his future in his own hand.

But Jesus is telling a different story. He says that those who have no power and those who choose to give up their power are the ones who inherit the earth, which could also be translated as "the land." The people sitting before him as he recites his poem of macarisms are certainly not landowners. They are most likely what we would consider today to be sharecroppers, working the land for a wealthy owner, who didn't need to get his hands dirty.

Richard Rohr says that when Jesus assures the crowd that those who are meek will inherit the land, he's saying it with a bit of a wink. The crowd would have recognized this. And they would have caught that he is quoting from Psalm 37:11: "the humble shall have the land for their own." Sometimes that word from the Psalms, which was written in Hebrew—*anavim*—is translated as "humble." And sometimes it's translated as "meek," "poor," or "afflicted."[10]

Jesus uses a psalm that his listeners would have recognized, all while knowing that every ordinary person in the crowd, most of the people sitting at his feet while he taught that day, would have felt vindicated in hating their landlords. Those who literally "possessed the land" did so almost entirely through violent control and oppression. Those who worked the fields were taxed a large portion of the profits of their hard work, while the landlords sat on their riches.[11] When Jesus offers land to the nonviolent, he is speaking a language that makes no sense. The violent own the land, obviously. The violent keep the land by wielding their power.

This is still the way the world works. The rich get richer by wielding violence, and the ones who do the hard labor walk away with barely enough food for the table. But Jesus is interested in a new way of being human. He is interested in bringing God's dream into reality. And in God's dream for the world, the land belongs

75

to those who choose not to wield their power. The land belongs to the humble, to the nonviolent.

"*Makarioi* are the powerless ones," Jesus says. "They shall have the earth as an inheritance." They will recognize that the earth has always been theirs. He is getting at something essential to the spiritual life: our ownership is temporal.[12] According to the psalmist, human beings are like the leaves of grass, here for a moment and then, *poof*, gone. We're all stewards here, and the land remains long after we've become the dust we came from. Only the divine one possesses it. In God's dream for the world, possession is an illusion. When we humble ourselves, when we release our hands from all that we have tried to control and cling to, we discover that those who possess the land are the ones living under the illusion. But the ones who release their power and the ones who never had power to begin with inherit the really real.

Maybe on the hillside as Jesus preaches those words, perhaps some of his listeners are beginning to experience that inheritance. The disciples, who most likely lived in poverty, with no land to their names, had chosen an even smaller life than the ones they had known before they came across their rabbi. They had chosen to release their control, their careers, perhaps even their financial security, and to begin walking the countryside with the unsanctioned religious leader. The disciples left the homes they lived in and went out on the road, joining their wandering spiritual guide. They essentially turned whatever rafts they had around and started paddling upstream. "Come and die" was Jesus's pep talk. And somehow, inexplicably, they agreed to try.

And this feels like the secret Jesus is letting his listeners in on: the power we're born into and the power we gain throughout our lives are a mirage. In the really real, power can only be shared. This is a radical way of living in community. It's Gabriela walking Ace to class. His reliance on her help allows him to be open to the give-and-take of relationship. And her openness to his differences teaches her to live gently in the world. Because of Ace's need and lack of security, his presence invites those in his orbit into a kind of mutual reciprocity. His way of living teaches meekness—the upside-down possibility that when we let go of the power we hoard, power grows wide enough to share. When the few in power release their hold on the land, everyone has space to spread out and flourish. Meekness is the way toward an earth where we live in peace, where resources are shared, where everyone has enough.

• • •

I have spent most of my life assuming that when I finally make myself good, by which I mean perfect, I will be enough. This is a mirage, a wobbly lie of a vision, which somehow has settled into the core of my self-experience. The mirage says my power relies on how I prove myself. And anxiety is the currency I pay when I believe it.

I worry most at night. If I wake to the sound of the dog shuffling from one side of the room to the other or the echo of a car door thudding into place outside the window, I feel my jaw tense back into a state of muscular alert. It has been vigilant since I received my first B in elementary school, my first recognition of personal failure. My eight-year-old inner critic awoke in a dark and uncertain room of my interior self's fortress, promising that she would never allow that kind of failure to sneak up on us again. I set my jaw, as they say. It relaxes a bit while I sleep, but when I wake, it springs back to its natural state, and so does my eight-year-old self, promising that she won't let weakness hurt us.

There are always things to worry about. Tasks to be completed, emails to return. But often my fears are a visual loop of what might happen, what has happened. I imagine Ace at his desk as his classmates move around him, speaking to each other, working on projects he is not a part of. He spins that pool ring on the table, watching it move around and around. Once a dentist said to me, "Isn't it so sad?"

"Sad?" I asked.

· "The way they see the world. Autistic people."

I stared at her, flabbergasted. Did she actually just say this in front of my son while staring into my eyes? "No," I said. "I don't think it's sad." I wrote a strongly worded email, and we found a new dentist.

In my mind at night, he spins the ring around and around, and I watch him, acknowledging that I believe this is beautiful, my son and the way he sees the world. And also, this terrifies me. I can put on a brave face when I talk about his neurodivergence or his disabilities, and when I do, I become an alternate version of myself: the advocate-mother—courageous, well spoken, intentional—making a path for my son in a world that wants to ignore him. But in the middle of the night, as my anxiety becomes a bull ramming its head into the fragile cage of my ribs, I am tender. I want to be grateful, but I spend the minutes wondering how long the children in his classroom will choose to be kind to him. Ace isn't yet able to reciprocate friendship. He can't intentionally communicate beyond smiles, frowns, or outward displays of high fives, hugs, and holding hands. Will the kids who love him now be present for him in the future? I long for Gabriela and Amelia to make room for him at the cafeteria table in middle school. I want Enzo to high-five Ace in the hall when they're both in seventh grade. But I fear that my nonspeaking son will, by that time, be segregated at the far side of the giant middle school, out of sight and out of mind, powerless to build the community he needs.

It's the powerless who most need community, and that is the real miracle of meekness. Jesus's promise that meekness leads to flourishing becomes most real when the community is willing to stand together in spaces where the world is not equitable or right, sharing a common calling to see the world made whole. This is an invitation to a better world, what some of the great Black theological voices of the twentieth century, including Howard Thurman and Martin Luther King Jr., called beloved community.[13]

• • •

Episcopal priest and author Stephanie Spellers explains that beloved community is the profound and simple work of helping one another become everything God dreams of us becoming. She says you don't have to be religious to long for this. It's both natural and compelling.[14] Beloved community isn't a watered-down version of performative racial harmony, not a soda commercial in which people of all colors hold hands across the world. Instead, she says, it's a muscular and absolute vision of the dream of God, the vision Jesus was introducing to his followers. Under God's reign on earth, love is not a squishy ideal. It's a way of being neighbors together. It's a way of living for the good of everyone.[15] And the only way to accomplish that lofty goal is to reject our dependence on and submission to the power we've been taught to hoard for ourselves, release it, and begin to work toward the common good.

The great theologian and civil rights leader Howard Thurman wrote that when we value love and justice for our neighbor, we "work for the creation of a society where it is easier for people to be good."[16] As Ace's peers learn to accept his atypical behaviors and sounds, perhaps they will grow into adults who will continue to choose relationship with those who live with less power. I dream that this exposure to my son might open their minds and spirits to see the glory of all humanity, to experience the weaknesses and limitations of others as something good, beautiful even, and to see their own limitations in the same way.

Meekness invites us to recognize the power, the skill, and the gifts we bring to the world in one hand, while in the other it acknowledges that our power, skills, and gifts can never determine our intrinsic worth. It's that sense of our own value, our own belovedness, that gives us courage to release our need for striving or competing.[17] It's as simple as Jesus's greatest commandments: We love God. We love others. We love ourselves.

And maybe that's how the land becomes our own. When we can learn to set aside our striving, our hands are free to receive it, not because we've earned it but because it has always been ours.

4

For the Ones Who Long for Justice

Makarioi are the ones who long for justice that restores and dignifies. They will be filled with whole and mutually dependent love.

JULY 2015 (ACE, THREE MONTHS OLD)
CONNECTICUT

We lean over the pack 'n play in a dark room at Chris's dad's house. August is a newly minted seven-year-old whose past two weeks have been filled with swimsuits and slabs of sunscreen. We're on an extended trip to the East Coast, where the sun shines hot in the summer and grandparents and aunts and uncles seem to be waiting in every town across the mid-Atlantic states.

It's afternoon. August has followed me and his baby brother from the pool in the backyard to the guest room, where Ace's travel crib is set up. I'm in a towel and swimsuit. I change Ace's diaper on the bed while August watches.

"Do you remember how to swaddle him?" I ask.

"Yeah," he whispers. Ace is awake, but the lights are dim and the curtains pulled. When Brooks was born, August was only three. Now he's alert and aware and is taking his role as big brother seriously.

I pick Ace up while August lays the soft cotton blanket onto the bed in a diamond shape. I show him how to fold down the top like a triangle to make space for Ace's head.

"See, we lay him down just like this." I set Ace's full, fresh body on top of the blanket. "Now pull the right side all the way to here." August tucks the corner of the blanket under Ace's right arm a little haphazardly. I tighten it, snuggling it in place. "Then what do you do?"

"The bottom part," August answers.

"Yep," I say as he pulls the blanket up to Ace's chest. Ace's eyes follow us. He's sleepy, but he's watching. He loves to watch his brothers. "And then the left side, all the way across," I say as August pulls the blanket across Ace's middle. I help move the final corner into place and tuck it around Ace's left shoulder.

"There," I whisper, "snug as a bug in a rug."

"Let's sing Ace's song, Mama."

"Okay, you start."

"I am Acey! I am Acey!" August sings. I join him. "I'm a sweet little boy. I am Acey! I am Acey! And I bring so much joy."

Ace has just learned to smile at thirteen weeks, and he's alert enough to open his gummy mouth at us.

"Acey, you're so sweet," August whispers. He doesn't have his r sound yet, so his "you're" sounds like "yough."

I lift Ace up, swaddled tight, and put his head in the crook of my left arm, my right hand on his back. "Sh, sh, sh," I whisper. "It's time for night night, buddy."

"Mama," August whispers. "I want you to pray for Ace."

"Okay." I lay his brother down inside the crib. "What do you want me to pray for?"

"I'm worried about his dreams," he says, looking down from his perch over the pack 'n play. "I just don't want him to have a bad dream. And I'm worried he'll have a good dream, then he might be sad when he wakes up and it isn't real."

"That makes sense," I say. "But maybe he'll have a good dream and he'll wake up and it is real. Maybe he'll dream about being at Grandpa's house with his big brothers, and Mommy wrapping him up tight, and us singing a song to him."

August looks at me like I definitely don't understand how dreams work. He has suffered from nightmares since he was two years old. He still talks about the very scary walrus that entered his closet that year. "Maybe," he says skeptically. He stands, thinking for a beat.

"And pray for his Down sin drum."

I'm surprised and turn from my spot beside the travel crib to look at the little boy beside me.

"What should I pray for his Down syndrome, buddy?"

"Pray that it won't hurt him."

I take a breath in, feeling the weight of those words. When Ace was born thirteen weeks ago, Chris and I weren't sure how to tell our boys about Down syndrome. They'd never known anyone with the condition. How could they understand what it would mean for their baby brother, what it would mean for their lives? When we were given Ace's prenatal diagnosis, I wept first for them, for the responsibilities they'd have to hold, for the challenges they had never asked for. Would they have the kind of supportive, loving relationship with Ace that Chris and I have with our siblings? How would it feel to hear some kid in their class make fun of their little brother? Would one of them feel pressure to care for their brother when Chris and I one day couldn't?

In those early weeks, when other parents at August's school would ask about how Ace was doing as I walked my second grader into class, August would tug on my sleeve, excited. "Mom, tell them about the Down sin drum!" Something was wonderful and important about his brother.

Ten days after Ace was born, I took him for his second echocardiogram, performed this time outside my body. I gently placed all six pounds of him on the cold exam table as the cardiologist strapped electrodes to his tiny chest, his bare body uncertain why it had been removed from my warm arms. I held his hands, stroked his legs, and stared at the computer screen beside the table, praying that the echocardiogram results we had received while Ace was in utero would hold true and his heart was okay. A prayer that he wouldn't be among the 50 percent of people with Down syndrome born with conditions that require open heart surgery. But soon I moved from fear to wonder: I was seeing inside him, and on the screen his heart looked like a magic forest, the fluttering of his atriums and ventricles swaying from side to side. I heard myself laugh. He was alive.

When August asks me to pray for Ace's Down syndrome, I wonder what he means. Of course, I can list all the medical fears, everything that can go wrong in a body with one extra copy of the twenty-first chromosome, every cell in every part of his body marked by this excess. And then I think of my one lucky egg that formed him, the chance that this one survived of all the eggs, all the months of my life. That this child was the one my body made. Like all of us, tender, original, miraculous.

What am I afraid of? I look at August, who has leaned over the travel crib, his hand gently pressed against Ace's swaddled belly. *Pray that it won't hurt him.*

I know that, despite all the medical fears, despite the struggle of those first few weeks to get him strong enough to latch on and breastfeed, despite concerns over his weight gain and calorie intake in these first few months—a challenge that will continue through all the early years of his life—the thing I fear most is Ace's real life. The life he'll have outside our family. The life he'll have at school, in his community, in his eventual workplace. The life he'll have in a world that doesn't believe in his value.

"God," I pray, "help Ace have a cozy nap. Help him feel all our love and know that he belongs to our family." August squeezes my hand and looks up at me. "And we pray for his Down syndrome. That it won't hurt him."

SPRING 2018
SAN FRANCISCO

I let out the breath I've been holding next to Chris in the car. It's raining outside. We've just arrived at the early childhood special education services for the city school district, a small outpost of an office building in an old school far from the district's main offices. This is our second meeting with the special education administrators. The first ended when we couldn't reach an agreement over Ace's placement in the pre-K program. Now Chris and I are walking into this meeting still unwilling to agree to the plan previously presented. We've been prepping for this meeting for months. I've sat through several "How to prepare for your child's first Individualized Education Plan" trainings at various disability support groups and conferences. I've researched online. And

85

we've hired an advocate to help us. We see her pull up in the parking space near us.

"You think we should pray?" I ask Chris.

"I think we've prayed a lot," he says, and still he takes my hand and says, "Take care of our boy."

I don't close my eyes. I stare straight ahead at the single-story brick building while he finishes with "And help us be brave."

It shouldn't feel like we're going into a courtroom, but it does. When children with disabilities turn three years old, they're automatically evaluated, labeled with official diagnoses, and placed in the school system. This fall Ace will start preschool in whatever school and classroom these conversations determine for him. We have been meeting about the goals the district will create for him, the kinds of supports and in-school therapies he will require, and the type of classroom he will most thrive in. We made it clear in our previous meeting with the district's representatives that we believe the best placement for him is in an inclusive setting. Inclusive classrooms aren't a new thing in San Francisco. There is more than one pre-K program in which kids with and without disabilities share a classroom space, along with dual teachers, one with credentials to teach general education and one trained for special education. These classrooms also have aides assigned to provide support. We're asking that Ace be given the chance to learn in this kind of classroom.

But Ace doesn't fit the description of a child who gets placed in an inclusive setting. His needs are too great. He's nonspeaking, not successfully stacking blocks (yes, they tested this), not playing pretend (they tested this too), and not showing signs of receptive communication, by which professionals mean he struggles to understand and respond to verbal questions and prompts. School districts are like everything else in our culture, run by the money machine. Inclusive practices are more expensive for a student like Ace. Supporting a child with a lot of needs in a classroom where not every child has those needs has a bigger dollar sign, and unfortunately, those of us who have read the research that inclusion better prepares young people with intellectual disabilities for social, emotional, and intellectual success are most often asked to bring in a lawyer or an advocate to force the hand of the system. That's what we're doing.

We sit at the table, each of us given a working document about my son, which lists in detail the various evaluations performed on my twenty-four-pound three-year-old, and a long list of his developmental deficits. In fact, the system's evaluations of his physical, emotional, and communicative skills are not designed to measure his skills at all. This list is only about lack, where he is missing the traditional developmental milestones. I will hear educators and legal experts talk about the reality of deficit-based measurements in the special education system many times following this experience. It's a shame, people say. If only we could measure in a more positive way. But the reality is that the public school system in the United States was not created for people with disabilities. A free and appropriate public education for kids like Ace wasn't made the law of the land until 1975, four years before I was born. And the system is still playing catch-up.

So, as it is for every child who enters the educational system with a disability, my son's weaknesses are printed out and discussed around the table, just as one might discuss a company's lack of profit shares at a board meeting. Cold, hard reality. Here's what your child cannot do. Read it in red ink.

The woman who tested Ace on his cognitive skills sits across the table from me. She is unimpressed that I want Ace to be in a different classroom than the one he was originally assigned. She tells me that his skills are not compatible with the requirements for inclusion. I blink to control my tears. Crying about the list in front of me is not going to help my son's case. I remind myself that she is beholden to a bottom line. There is only so much money to go around in the school district, and Ace's list of deficits looks like any list of deficits: a drain on resources, not the kind of investment she is free to make. After all, he doesn't speak, can't stack blocks, and hasn't yet learned to hold a crayon.

"*Makarioi* are the ones who long for justice that restores and dignifies," Jesus proclaims to the crowd in Matthew 5. In Luke's version, he blesses not the ones whose desire for righteousness is like hunger but those who are literally hungry and thirsty, physically affected by a world in which food is hoarded by the wealthy while the impoverished go without the sustenance they need for life. Once again, the physicality of Luke's version of the Beatitudes can feel mean-hearted. How dare Jesus ask those who are hungry to see themselves as blessed? Our typical translation of blessing can feel like a pseudo-spirituality, a nice pat on the head for those who are suffering the very real effects of injustice.

But if, as theologian and New Testament professor Jonathan T. Pennington suggests, the pattern Jesus follows in the Beatitudes is based on the Greco-Roman virtue tradition of macarisms, then he is joining his own words to an already existing tradition of exploring what it means to be a whole and flourishing person. That means that Jesus is not offering spiritual platitudes at all.[1] He is offering a congratulations of sorts, a statement about the character of those who live with the suffering of injustice: You are whole if you are hungry. You are thriving if you are thirsty, even if the world says you are the least among us. When you suffer, God is especially near to you.[2]

There are several times in this meeting when I try to speak but can't, when I'm so grateful for the advocate sitting beside me who says what I mean to say, who presents our case, not based on Ace's skill set but based on the law, that every child in the United States qualifies for a free and appropriate education. And based on evidence, inclusion is appropriate. When Ace was born, I was terrified of the list that now sits before me—his limits, pulled apart, analyzed, and judged—all the ways he doesn't meet our culture's values of bright, able, and impressive. I don't want strangers handing me these test results, their hard data that my son is not enough, that his lack of development makes him unworthy of the classroom where statistics tell me he will most thrive. There's a desperation in my gut, something I've rarely experienced in my middle-class, white, straight, cis life: injustice.

I have rarely known what it is to be rejected, to be denied opportunity. But in this moment, I experience a power that has control over the future of my son, a power that refuses to see his dignity beyond the cold, hard facts, and I feel righteous anger bubbling in my chest. I recognize that I live in a world that has rejected his personhood.

When Matthew uses the Greek word *dikaiosunē* in Jesus's blessings, the word we often translate as "righteousness," it's usually taken religiously, as if this is a blessing for those who do good, or those who want to do good, who make an effort to avoid sin. But *dikaiosunē* means both "righteousness" and "justice." Righteousness comes from the Old English word *rihtwīs*, which joins together "right" and "wise."[3] It involves right relationship with our neighbor, or even our seemingly coldhearted district special education representative. And it requires wisdom. It's a word that points us not toward moral superiority but toward restorative justice, the wise and righteous treatment of the beings with whom we share our resources.

In Matthew's version, this blessing on those who long for righteousness is a statement of flourishing for all of us who choose to move with courage toward humility so we can see beyond our own needs and experiences. Only then do we become people of inclusion, those who work for the wholeness and dignity of others. While the first three blessings of Jesus's poem are given to those who are poor in spirit, those who mourn, and those who are meek, this blessing offers all of Jesus's listeners the opportunity to move from a place of passive experience to active participation. Jesus invites his followers on the hill to choose a new way of living in the world, and here in this meeting, with a printout of Ace's deficits in my hand, I receive that invitation as well. Gregory Boyle says that the Beatitudes are not a spirituality but a geography that "tells us where to stand."[4] This is how we get to the flourishing life: We work to make things right and just. We long for it. We hunger.

Whole and flourishing are you who are hungry to see the world made right, those of you who thirst for right relationship and wisdom. There is a connection between hunger and holiness, between longing and feeding, between a yearning to see the world made right and the courage that strives for justice. To move toward beloved community, we must first recognize how often we instinctively rely on systems of power and money out of a longing for comfort and safety instead of choosing something much riskier—to live and work for the common good.

Andy Crouch, who writes and thinks about issues of faith and culture, describes our dependence on power and money as "mammon," the Aramaic word Jesus uses later in his Sermon on the Mount to describe "a rival to God, an alternative Lord."[5]

It's often translated into English as simply "money," but it has a bigger, more layered meaning. It's significant that when the gospel writers Matthew and Luke preserved the teachings of Jesus, translating the original Aramaic into Greek—the language their readers knew best—they chose to leave the Aramaic word *mammon*. The word was, and still is, compelling.

"Mammon is not simply money but the anti-God impetus that finds its power in money," Crouch explains, describing it as a spiritual principality that is twisted and manipulative, a power that exists beyond our understanding of ideology or systematic structures, "a will at work in history." Above all, he says, mammon allows us to experience power without relationship, resulting in a culture in which we no longer depend on one another to meet our basic needs, a society that devalues personhood.[6] In other words, when mammon is given free reign, we begin to live without the beating heart of justice: relationship, kinship, goodness. Power and money take the place of mutual dependence, and the people who suffer are the ones last in line for the power, the ones Jesus says matter most.

There is never enough mammon to go around. Those who get it hoard it, and the rest suffer. When we choose the powers of mammon over the good of the community, we also lose personhood, the particular value of every human. And for those of us who hoard mammon, the poor, the hungry, and the othered all become subgroups we think of from time to time but rarely encounter.

This understanding of mammon also has the power to speak to issues of racial injustice. For those of us who have knowingly or unknowingly benefited from the long history of whiteness and its deep-rooted partnership with power, Jesus's *makarioi* invites us to recognize how white culture, or what author and researcher Isabel Wilkerson calls America's "dominant caste," has aligned itself with mammon's power over the course of US history, resulting in an imbalance of resources.⁷ When we who benefit from whiteness allow the inequality of the past to continue into the present, we not only succumb to the power of mammon but also impoverish ourselves of full relationships—beloved community—with our neighbors who are Black, Indigenous, or People of Color.

Stephanie Spellers summarizes Howard Thurman's vision of beloved community as a "radical reorientation of self to God and to other." This is how we strive to denounce the distorting work of mammon in our lives across culture and society. This is the way we move toward what Spellers calls "a total reversal of empire."⁸ The practice of meekness invites those of us who have benefited from power without relationship to recognize how mammon has privileged us above others, how we have lived under its authority. When our eyes begin to open to mammon's power in the world, the injustices of the world no longer seem distant and untouchable. To benefit from the power of racial, economic, or ableist injustices is to feed the monster of mammon.

Jesus is giving his followers a way out of the monster's control. The wise and fully alive people, Jesus says to his listeners on the hill, are the ones who are hungry and thirsty, the ones who long for something better than mammon's false strength and twisted influence in our systems of power. The flourishing life belongs to the ones who work toward an ecosystem of wholeness. To hunger and thirst for a world where every human is treated with equity is to live in a constant push and pull of desire and struggle. It's uncomfortable to long for change in a world that moves toward transformation generation by generation, bits at a time. To embrace the kind of longing that calls for the world to change is to live with hope. Injustice never sleeps, and neither can our belief that the work of God is always a slow unfolding of goodness in the world.

Here in this meeting, I want to reject the special education staff as my enemies, as people who don't understand the value of my son's life, who have failed to read the latest articles about education and Down syndrome. But I know we're all living in mammon's distorted value system. This is why people with intellectual disability have lived almost fully relegated to the outside of our communities—taught in the classroom at the edge of the school building, bused to the specialized school in the next town over, and eventually sent to adult caregiving facilities on the outskirts of the city. Mammon distorts our vision of one another's full humanity so that we miss the personhood of the individual in front of us who may not speak, who may not control their bodily functions, who may not contribute to the local economy. Much of our culture has been trained to see little of my son's value beyond dollar signs, the time he demands, and the resources he requires.

The opposite of mammon is the heart of beloved community, "ordinary embodied human existence."[9] When Jesus blesses the ones who long for justice that restores and dignifies, he calls them to reject any way of living that prioritizes power over relationship. He invites his followers to choose dependence on one another above the allure of economic autonomy. It makes sense then that the hungry, the thirsty, and those who are weak in the eyes of the world are living outside the false comforts of the system of mammon. When we begin to think of that system as anything that separates us from loving relationship with one another, Jesus's blessing for those who hunger and thirst becomes a blessing for all of us. Those who have been denied beloved community because the system of mammon has rejected their personhood, and those of us who have experienced ease and comfort because we have fit the system's distorted definition of value, can choose to work toward freedom. We are all invited to flourish in the ordinary, mutually dependent way of Jesus.

Jesus's words invite all of us to transform the systems we live within. Those of us with food in our fridges can refuse to accept a world where systemic hunger exists. Those of us who, like me, have always benefited from white majority status can reject any system that prioritizes our lives over the lives of our neighbors who are Black, Indigenous, or People of Color. And we who rely on our intellectual abilities to meet our daily needs can choose to seek out the places where the intellectually disabled have been cast aside and turn our neighborhoods and churches into places for everyone in our communities.

Stephanie Spellers says that though beloved community is still only a dream for us, "for God, it's reality."[10] It takes faith to move toward God's dream, and that movement begins by freeing ourselves from the hold of mammon in our lives, recognizing that we can flourish only when our spirits are whole enough to see the wholeness of the other.[11]

The school district representatives don't budge in the meeting. In fact, it won't be until three months later, after Chris and I write a letter threatening a lawsuit, that a space for Ace in the inclusion classroom becomes available. We'll recognize how few children with disabilities have parents with the time and resources necessary to engage in that kind of struggle. As I leave the meeting holding the official documentation of all my child's limitations, my chest feels like it's been scraped out. I drop Chris off at his shuttle stop and drive to my friend Leah's house, where Ace has been playing with his buddy Jonah. Ace is in their small, paved backyard, bouncing a ball with Leah while Jonah digs dirt with his toy digger. When I see Ace pass the ball to Leah, I think of the document's notation that he is "unable to complete the instruction to pass the ball." I smile, recognizing that Ace is fully capable of passing a ball to someone he knows and loves. Who can blame him for refusing to follow the instructions of the stranger who performed the receptive language exam? Here, with the people who love him, he does this freely.

Leah's son, Jonah, was born two days after Ace. They've shared a birthday party all three years of their lives. And every month, Jonah's typical development reminds me that Ace's way of being will always be distinct, divergent, from his friend's growth and progression.

Jonah pours dirt into his toy's big scoop while he gives voice to the digger and backhoe, who are having an important conversation about the building they're constructing. Ace and Jonah can't play this game together. And the only shame in this reality is the shame society puts on my son for the differences in his development. I don't have words yet for my fierce defense of Ace's personhood, or the force of mammon's power in his life, but I feel the injustice in my body. Leah sees my tears and pulls me in for a hug. She has also watched our boys drift further and further from each other developmentally.

"Ace! Ace!" Jonah yells. "Come see what I did." Ace ignores his friend and squats to watch an ant crawl past his foot.

JULY 2015
CONNECTICUT

After August and I pray for Ace beside the pack 'n play at my father-in-law's house, I take a walk around the block, listening to a podcast interview with a musician whose daughter was born with Down syndrome just a year ago. She's reflecting on her fear, her grief, and the ways her sorrow has turned to joy in this first year of her child's life. As I listen, I sense that I am afraid not because of my baby's diagnosis but because of how the world sees it. I stay with that thought for a bit, then ask myself a question that will remain with me, challenging me to wrestle with and expand my answers for years to come: What makes us human?

In the past, I might have pointed to our ability to think critically, to problem solve. Or maybe humanity requires a human body—two arms, two legs, ten toes. Am I human because I am conscious? Am I human because I can speak? What will I believe about Ace's humanity if he never speaks, never thinks critically or problem solves? Who determines his humanity?

I walk past the manicured Connecticut lawns and the two-hundred-year-old stone church, then turn the corner, where the cars wait anxiously for the light to change. How will I define my child's worth in a world that demands proof of his value?

I'll come to recognize the answer in the concept of personhood. We are valuable because we *are*. Eventually, I'll think about Jesus's promise of flourishing to the ones who hunger for justice—that they will find themselves filled all the way to overflowing—and I'll wonder if that filling is actually the gift of love, the gift of worth and value, the gift of mutually dependent relationships.

"What made you decide to keep him?" an acquaintance asked me eight weeks prior. We were in the school courtyard at drop-off. Our boys, buddies from school, shot imaginary slime at each other and ran past us toward their second-grade line. Ace was asleep on my chest, wrapped in the stretchy, handmade Moby wrap my sister-in-law had sent me. We were standing side by side, the foggy gray sky thick around us.

He might as well have asked, "What made you decide his life was worthy of existence? What made you decide his incomplete humanity deserved your time and mothering?"

I was astonished at first. Who would ask this of a new mom? And then, as I began to experience moving through the world with my son, his face touched by Down syndrome, on full display to strangers, I realized that many people find this question acceptable, even necessary. We've been trained to value our own worth based on what we produce, how we perform in our studies or careers, the sign of having raised good humans often determined by how they are "contributing" to culture or to the economy. When a person fails to produce, perform, or contribute, they become a drain on society, the money sign above their head flashes. This is an unspoken reality, something we rarely give voice to—except in jokes about the stupid, the lazy, or the ones who ride the short bus—accepting as reality that those who drain resources are less human than the rest of us. All of us who have lived subject to mammon have been trained to question the humanity of my son, even if we're too polite to say so out loud.

Why did you keep him? On the school blacktop, my newborn wrapped against my body, my answer was weaker than I wanted it to be. "We wanted him," I said, my hand resting on his bottom, where his legs curled under him in the same fetal position he had held for nine months. My body was suddenly on high alert, protecting his right to exist. The rest of my words stuck in my throat. *I wanted my baby. This is my baby.*

Now, as I walk the neighborhood, knowing that back at my father-in-law's house Chris and our two older boys are splashing in the pool while Ace sleeps in the dark afternoon shade of the guest bedroom, I have yet to make sense of this new world I've joined. I don't have language for what it might mean to live in an economy of wholeness, where there is enough to go around—enough sustenance, enough opportunity, enough value. A world in which those who hunger and thirst for food and drink and those who choose, in solidarity with the suffering, to hunger and thirst for righteousness, will be filled and overflowing.

It will take me years to come to Jesus's words and find my son inside them, to recognize that Jesus has always been inviting us to remake culture in a way that centers the personhood of all: of the weak and rejected, of all who are subject to impoverished conditions, ableism, racism, and sexual-orientation and gender-based discrimination. These are blessed, not by any false religious artifice but by a sturdy wholeness, a label of dignity from a God who does not distinguish our value based on the system of mammon. Those who deserve justice are flourishing because in God's dream they are the ones who show us the way of mutual dependence, a way in which relationship is never power based, a whole and life-giving way of needing one another.

Ace, I will learn, will not be hurt by his Down syndrome. He'll be hurt by the way our culture encounters, judges, and pities his Down syndrome. But in the flourishing life, the life Jesus invites his listeners to receive on the hill that day near the Sea of Galilee, the ones rejected by society become the gifts, the ones whose very lives free us from the burden to keep up with the culture of power, money, and success.

It turns out that "keeping him" will rescue me from the accomplishment culture I was born into. Ace's life invites me to reject my desires for power, my need for accomplishment, so that the really real can begin to heal my dangerous perceptions around value, inviting me to a bigger longing, a kind of justice in which we are all restored to dignity and the wholeness that is the dream of God.

5

For the Ones Who Give Mercy

Makarioi are the ones who give mercy. They will receive in turn what they have offered in love.

August, Chris, and I have been in family therapy together on and off for a few years. School continues to be overwhelming for August, and we have sought diagnoses to help explain his struggle to walk into the school building in moments of panic or complete his homework when it feels difficult. The experts have given him the same diagnosis as mine: generalized anxiety disorder. He is terrified, and my job is to help him be at peace in a world that, to me, seems just as scary as August's body says it is.

This spring we try something new. The therapist we've been working with recommends a colleague of hers who helps kids learn to cope using breathing techniques and age-appropriate meditations. August and I meet with her four Saturdays in a row.

August plays with putty while Sarah asks him questions about his moments of overwhelm. "What does it feel like inside you when you don't want to get out of the car outside of school?" and "When you yell and throw things when Mom asks you to wash your hands, what do you wish she could understand about you?"

They draw pictures. He has been into comics for a while now and is always fascinated with scary tales, craving them by day and fixating on them by night. So, though August hasn't grown up in a church setting that emphasizes Satan or tales of the devil, when his nine-year-old self looks for language to describe the tightness in his chest, the thump of dread that attempts to control what his mind knows he can't, he names it Satan Strawberry.

"So tell me about your drawing," Chris says later.

"It's a comic."

"Okay, your comic." We've just walked in the door in time for lunch. Chris and Ace are playing on the floor of the living room. August is holding the picture he drew that morning in his hand. He walks over to his dad and holds it out.

"That's me." He points. "And that's Satan Strawberry. And that's what happens to me when Satan Strawberry wakes up."

The paper around the strawberry with the angry face is filled with scribbles and lightning bolts. A strawberry bursts from the sketched boy's chest. Its eyes are wide, and bolts shoot from its hands.

"That's pretty scary, buddy."

August looks at his dad, annoyed.

"Of course it's scary. It's Satan Strawberry."

He walks to his room and closes the door, letting the comic fall to the ground in the hallway.

The hardest part of parenting a kid who is terrified of life is learning to speak that child's language. Parenting in the wrong language feels like chaos. In the wrong language, the tender words I utter from my most gentle parenting self or the lullabies I sing in the shadows of his room turn into words floating near my child's body, never quite received. I've spent years desperate to say the right thing, attempting to reflect back to my child that his fears are real and difficult, just like the therapist taught me. I always feel that even my most careful attempts still somehow miss him.

"Tell me about your family," Sarah the therapist asks the first time we meet with her. August describes Brooks, how his younger brother likes LEGOs and dress-up and talks in silly voices and pretends to play air guitar whenever music is on. "Mom is nice, even though she yells sometimes. She likes to sing in the car and makes really good burritos because she's from Texas. Dad is the best pancake maker in the world because he makes them thin so you can eat as many of them as you are old. He also yells sometimes."

"What about Ace? What's he like?"

August describes his brother, almost two, who can say three words: "Dada"; Ezra (our cat), pronounced "Ehda"; and August, pronounced "Ahda."

"That must be pretty special that he says your name when he doesn't say very many things."

"Yeah. Well, I'm his big brother."

"Yes, and he probably really wants to be like you. Does he play with you?"

"Sometimes. When my friends are over and we're outside, he looks out the window really cute because he wants to play too. And we jump on the trampoline. Well, he can't jump yet, but he sits. And Brooksie and I jump."

"What about when you're angry and upset? What does Ace do then?"

August shifts uncomfortably on the couch. He doesn't like talking about the moments when he can't regulate his emotions, when he screams or stomps or shuts down. I used to call them tantrums, but, as he's gotten older, I've realized they are deeper and more painful to August than any lingo used to describe willful toddlers. These are panic attacks: something I, unfortunately, know all about. No matter how angry he appears, he is not in control. My job as his parent has always been to help him out of the chaos, to help him feel safe, instead of reacting with anger. Sometimes that feels impossible.

"Sometimes Ace is sad when I cry. He doesn't like it."

"That makes sense, doesn't it? It's hard to watch someone you love cry."

"Yeah, I guess so."

"What do you think Ace knows about you?"

"Like that I'm his brother?"

"Yes, and other things. Like how you talk and how you act when you're sad, and what you're good at, what makes him laugh."

"Oh, he likes it when Brooksie and I wrestle him on the bed. And we tickle him."

"Yeah, like that! What else does he know about you?"

"He knows that I will take care of him. He knows that I can read. He knows that I can ride a bike and do parkour."

"You do parkour?"

"Yeah, I'm really good." August looks at me for reassurance. The putty in his hands shifts from ball to snake to blob. I nod my head.

"It sounds like Ace knows you really well."

"Yep, and his hugs are the best ones. Better than anybody else's in my house. Besides the cat."

"Does it help when he hugs you if you're crying and upset?" the therapist asks.

August looks at me again. He and I have struggled through meltdowns; screaming matches; and tearful, body-regulating hugs on the floor of his room, at the playground, or on the hard ground of the blacktop outside of his school. We've both cried tears over what we can't control in each other. I had once imagined I would be a mom who would talk her kids into goodness with a few wise words, that I'd have children who would want to please me. And August has wished for a mom and dad who never scream in frustration when he slams a door or refuses to get in the car. He dreams of a mom and dad who don't stomp away for fear of losing control, a mom who doesn't cry for herself when she's supposed to be comforting him.

"Yep," August says, looking up and meeting her eyes. "I really like it when Ace gives me a hug."

The therapist readjusts in her seat across from the couch where August and I sit. "I wonder, August, if Ace might be like a superpower when you feel controlled by Satan Strawberry. It seems like he knows all the best things about you."

August nods his head.

"He knows what you're good at and what makes you funny. He knows that you love him and want to play with him. He knows all the really good things about you." August keeps his eyes on his lap, rolling the ball of putty in his hands, then squishing it. "What if when you feel out of control you can remember to see yourself the way Ace sees you? All the best parts of you?"

* * *

Before Jesus begins his sermon, Matthew gives us the tiniest bit of detail. Jesus sees the crowds, then begins climbing a hill, apparently making his followers work for their sermon. By the time he sits down to teach his disciples and followers that day, they've already put in a hike. After years on staff with youth ministry organizations, I know the goodness of tiring out your audience before they sit.

Did Jesus lead the procession or fall in with the drifters in the back? Did he chat on his way up the hill, hearing the stories of poverty, grief, and powerlessness—the stories of the ones to whom he'd later offer his blessings? I imagine him composing as he goes, praying wholeness and healing on the bodies around him, before he finally sits himself down and speaks the poem aloud. He blesses that crowd in a way that's almost indulgent— *this can be blessed, and this can be blessed*—subverting the reality of his listeners by inviting them into a deeper truth, a way of being human in the presence of the divine. His blessings insist that his listeners are actually closer to the dream of God than those who aren't suffering, closer than those who wield their power to control and manipulate.

Then, just as the crowd is likely wondering what he can possibly mean that anyone might flourish in the midst of poverty, grief, powerlessness, or the desire for a just world, Jesus presents yet another reversal.[1] He transitions from their limits and longings to a way of living *makarios*, the flourishing life. Thriving are the mercy givers in an unmerciful world.[2] Whole are those who learn to look with love.[3]

Mercy is learning to look with love. Maybe that was what Jesus was doing on his hike, before he ever sat down. Looking at the crowd with love, seeing what they were carrying into that day. I imagine he felt the weight of their expectations. They had come to hear him speak because word was getting around. This guy had something special to say. Did he worry he might not live up to

their hopes for him? Was he overwhelmed with wanting to transform the suffering of their lives? The most common Hebrew word
for "mercy" is *hesed*, which can be translated "self-giving, unconditional love."[4] In the Greek New Testament, the word translated
"mercy" is *eleos*, similar to the Greek word *eleēmosunē*, "gracious
deeds done for those in need." And also, surprisingly, a word for
the inarticulate sounds associated with suffering—"sighs, groans,
moans, sobs, and laments."[5]

It makes sense that Jesus would arrive at mercy in his fifth
blessing, right in the middle of his poem. Mercy is the overflow of
seeing people as they really are, in all their suffering, all their delight, all their possibilities. If Jesus had engaged with the stories
of those who walked with him all the way up that hill, I imagine
he would have recognized mercy as the beginning and the end
of their stories, both the groans of sorrow and the clarion call of
unconditional love. Maybe it's the same thing. To see another
person in truth is also, mysteriously, to love them. Whole and
honored are those who look with the eyes of love on those who
wail and groan. Because when we look with eyes of love, that love
comes back to us, a circular, *more real* way of seeing and acknowledging each other.

In the Old Testament, the psalmists call out for mercy in hope
that the divine might undo or heal what's broken.[6] But mercy is
also given as an attribute of God: "All the paths of the LORD are
mercy and truth," the psalmist writes.[7] I like that there's no mercy
without truth in that description. The truth described here is not
the kind of "truth" used to clobber, to put people in their place.
It's the kind of truth that reveals the core reality underneath all
we use to hide ourselves. This is the kind of truth that exists only
alongside mercy, that reveals itself only through love. As someone
who's experienced plenty of religious pretense—both my own

and the feigned Christian piety I've encountered in a lifetime of churchgoing—I have learned to cling to this. Real mercy, the kind that transforms, is true through and through.

Jesus is inviting his followers to claim this way of being, to become all mercy and truth with their very living. To somehow do what he is practicing in that moment, fresh off the hike up that hill. He looks on them and offers another way, a fledgling idea of a community in which the people turn toward their oppressors and reverse the story. "You have heard that it was said, 'Love your neighbor and hate your enemy.' But I tell you, love your enemies and pray for those who persecute you," Jesus would say later in that same sermon.[8] He speaks mercy and truth, and a wild belief that compassion and preemptive generosity might just have the power to transform the entire story we live inside.

Reversing the story begins with how we see one another. In the really real, practicing mercy is beholding the other in their deepest truth, who God created each of us to be beneath our egos, poses, and the destructive choices that add to the suffering of others. Mercy is the practice of remembering that the human we are encountering in every circumstance is "a being made in the divine image who is deeply loved."[9] Our darkness, our rage, and our destruction are not the truest things about us. And when we begin to see the reality of God's divine image in every soul, we live in what Frederick Bruner calls "the morality of extension, of width, of forgiving." Bruner describes this mercy as the work of *understanding* in its most basic form—standing under the other, putting oneself in a place so as to hold the other up.[10]

"Let mercy outweigh everything else in us," Saint Isaac of Syria said. "Let compassion be a mirror."[11] Jesus is inviting his followers to move past their suffering and into the true character of divine love. When we look with love, the really real inside us widens. We become the reversal, the blessing of God that actually grows out of merciful looking.

SPRING 2018
SAN FRANCISCO

Satan Strawberry sticks to August's gray-and-black wall for a year. At night, by the light that shines through the cracked-open door, I can see it taped beside the poster of *Jurassic Park*, across the room from the dream catcher on his bedpost ("just in case"). In this season, though he's nearly ten, he still struggles each night to fall asleep. I massage his body and speak the words that have become a kind of liturgy for us: "Relax your eyes," I say, touching my thumbs to his perfect eyebrows. "Relax your jaw." I feel my own face relax as I roll my fingers around his jawline. "Relax your shoulders. Relax your arms."

I make my way slowly, massaging his arms, then hands, then fingers, using the joint compression techniques Ace's occupational therapist taught me when he was a baby. I press gently into each joint, hoping that the pressure regulates his body enough to bring him out of panic and into the safety of rest. While I press down on elbows, wrists, and each individual finger, I remind August that he is safe in the dark. Sometimes, if we're lucky, he falls asleep before I even get to his legs. But sometimes he shakes himself awake, aware of something else nearby—a spooky character from a ghost story a friend once whispered at a sleepover, or perhaps the realization that he hasn't finished his homework. "Sh, honey," I say. And I start again: "Relax your eyes."

During that season, August is assigned the mandatory project every California kid creates in fourth grade: a replica of one of the California missions. This is a project he's supposed to have worked on at home over the course of a month, a project he refuses to talk about, crying at the thought of sitting down and making a list of what needs to happen. He and I have been through a lot of challenges when it comes to homework, so I tend to save my nagging for the big moments. But this project's deadline is getting close.

I walk toward his room, taking my deepest inhale. He's on his back, head propped up on pillows, looking at a book of comics. "It's time, buddy."

"No, it's not."

"Hey, I know it's not fun, but your project is due next Monday. And I know you haven't been doing it at school."

"I don't want to." He keeps his eyes on *Dog Man* and rolls over in his bed, his back to me.

"August, I want to help you. But you have to be willing to sit with me and talk through it."

He turns his body to look at me again. "I'm. Not. Going. To," he says, emphasis on each word. Then he turns again to face the wall. He's daring me to keep this up.

In my most fearful moments of mothering, I hold the words he's spoken in anger as proof of my failings. I didn't teach him to be kind. I didn't teach him to honor me or his responsibilities.

And in the moments I can remind myself of who my son is underneath his poses of power, I remember that he is growing and I'm the one helping him learn. His anger is just a feeling, not his character. After all, I'm still learning to control mine. And his response when he's stressed doesn't prove any of my fears of who he'll be as an adult.

This time, though, I'm on a train tracking straight to fear.

"Don't you speak to me like that."

August keeps his eyes on the wall.

"Hey. Look at me." He doesn't move. "Turn around and look at me!" I scream. The sound rises from the deepest part of my gut, the place where I am most afraid.

He turns toward me, all steel, his face calm and deliberate. "I'm not doing it," he says, refusing to raise his voice to the wild decibel where I've moved mine.

"Stand up and walk with me to the kitchen." I'm more growl than speech.

"I'm not doing it!" He joins me in the realm of what my mee-maw would have called "hollering" and throws *Dog Man* across the room. It barely misses me.

I stand in place for a beat. Then I roar. "Get up and pick up your book! Now, August. Pick it up!"

"I'm not doing it! I don't want to do it! I hate social studies and I hate this!" By now he's out of his bed, standing a foot from my flaming body, a pile of library books on the California missions just a few inches from his feet. He kicks. They scatter.

The therapists have taught me that in these moments I should say something gentle and calm like I've seen Daniel Tiger's mom do on TV. "Wow, you seem really upset, honey. It sure is hard to do a school project when you don't want to do it."

I'm not Daniel Tiger's mom.

"Yeah? You wanna kick the books? Think that'll get you through fourth grade?" He steps closer to me, his head almost as high as my cheek when we stand side to side—that long, lovely body I've touched nearly every day of his life, the hand I've held across streets and tickled in church. I don't dare touch him. It's strange how rage can make you forget how many times you kissed that belly, caressed that hair. "You're behind on your work, so this seems like a great plan. Why don't you climb back in your bed and read comics and see how your project turns out. Let's see if you're still yelling in two weeks."

I'm not sure why this particular child brings out the nastiest parts of me, my sarcasm the language of my sorrow. "Here's a plan!" I continue. "Fail fourth grade!" His face darkens, and I carry on. "I'm here. I want to help, and you don't care!" He keeps his eyes straight on mine, his foot inching toward one of the books he scattered the moment before. Kick.

"Oh, cool. Yeah. Kick the books!"

He's red and splotchy, and he speaks with a calm rage that confirms all my darkest suspicions. "I'm not doing it."

"Sure, of course. Because you get to control everything. Who cares what I say, right?" I stomp into the hallway. He slams the door behind me.

My own panic attacks have been coming off and on for a few years. Sometimes they show up when the kids and I run late or when my internal accusations of failure, particularly when it comes to Ace's weight, gain speed or volume. When the panic flames up from belly to throat, my pulse accelerates, my heart thwacking against my ribs until my mind releases and I float outside my skin and watch the woman with her head on the hardwood floor—like I'm doing right now. I'm not so much crying as panting like a wild thing. I'm like the boy on the other side of the door. Both of us out of control. Both of us wet-faced and monstered by our own insides.

I don't know how long it takes to come back to my body. Probably only a minute or so. And when I'm back, I find myself on my knees, the thought occurring that I can breathe, that I do know how to breathe, just like I practice each day in the quiet morning hour when I pray on the couch—long and slow around an imaginary box, across and down, across and up. These are the long breaths I've learned over time, my own weakness an embarrassment and a gift. Once upon a time, these moments brought only shame. Now, I am learning to look on my own poverty of mind with kindness. "You sweet thing," I imagine God says to me as I breathe. All love and truth. "I'm sorry," my mind whispers back.

All this time, in these ten minutes since August and I caught fire in the room beside theirs, Brooks and Ace have been playing, both of them used to our slamming doors and yelling voices. This has been our way for so long that August's younger brothers have found their own strategies for dealing with the normalcy of our fights. I shiver and breathe. In and out. "Love, not fear," I whisper to myself. Love, love, love.

I wanted to be a mom who raised gentle and curious kids, able to roll with a little spunk but always in control. A mom who sat at tables and helped build projects with the patience my dad had shown when, as my ten-year-old body was hiccuping tears, he seemed to pull out just the right thing: wood or Styrofoam or poster board, paint, and hot glue he'd saved for just this moment. Instead, I'm all tied up by my relentless struggle to be human in a world where too many feelings shake me out of safety and into a wild overwhelm that sends my right mind scattering, a world that makes highly sensitive kids build fourth-grade replicas of California missions. I remind myself that August is kind and funny and curious. He's only reacting to his own fear, just like I'm reacting to mine. He's afraid he will try and won't be enough. I'm afraid I've already tried and wasn't, afraid that a better parent would have nipped this problem in the bud long ago, afraid that my short temper will mark my son for life—already has. I'm afraid that my other kids have already been negatively shaped by the ways August and I scream, by the books he kicks and the breath I can't find on the other side of the door. I'm afraid that August will give up his curious mind and find dangerous ways to cope with his anxiety.

I hear feet pitter-patter toward me. Ace's toddler body. He's been walking only nine or ten months. He puts his hand on the back of my hair. "Aah," he says. I lift my head from the hardwood to his face. He stands before me in the hallway outside August's slammed door. I whisper, "It's okay, baby. We're okay."

I wipe my eyes, still waiting for the vibration below my ribs to settle. I shift my body from knees to seat, taking Ace into my lap. I smell his hair, and he wiggles out of my grasp, steadies himself back to standing. I want him to stay with me, to help me quiet my heart. Instead, he moves toward August's door, unlatched due to his forceful and unsuccessful slam.

Ace pushes it open. August sits on his rug, chest heaving, tears spread across his face. We look at each other. We are directly across from each other, my face as red and wet as his. Ace steps through the threshold, and August doesn't say a word. He stands and walks to his bed, falls on top of the gray quilt, his body still, his face in the pillow. Ace follows him and works to climb the twelve-inch height of the bed frame. He swings his extra-flexible leg to the top and manages the rest with just a little more effort.

I was afraid for both my older boys when I received the diagnosis for Ace. But I worried especially for August. His sensitivity to the world lives in his skin. How would he deal with the stares of strangers, recognizing that Ace's life was misunderstood? Could he handle loving a sibling who would be different, rejected, who may not get to experience life in the same way he had? What if he felt pressure to care for his brother and then rebelled?

What I hadn't planned for was this. I watch from the hall-way as Ace navigates his rear just close enough to August's back to offer a warm presence. He sits there, time insignificant, sometimes playing with the blanket, sometimes stimming with his voice. "Aah." I wipe my eyes and remember Satan Strawberry, whose power over both my son and me has exploded, resembling the scribbles August drew across that lined notebook paper just a year before. And I remember the therapist's suggestion: "I wonder, August, if Ace might be like a superpower?"

August turns to his side to face Ace, propping himself on his left elbow, wiping his eyes with his right hand. Ace stays still, fingering the blanket. Their eyes meet.

"What if when you feel out of control you can remember to see yourself the way Ace sees you? All the best parts of you?"

August sits up and reaches for his brother. Ace leans into him, keeping his hands to his side while August wraps his own arms around Ace. They lean against each other in the bed while I observe, my body heavy on the hard floor. I wish I were a better fit for August's needs, that my anxiety hadn't been passed to that boy I love who falls under its influence, mirror of his mother—all good intentions and reckless fear. But Ace has never minded Satan Strawberry. Or maybe he is simply more capable of seeing past him, of seeing his brother—and maybe his mother too—there beneath the fear and anger. I marvel at that toddler, perfectly willing to wait. And when August is ready, to lean in.

Maybe mercy is the real superpower here. Mercy is able to see beyond the roar of our overwhelm. Mercy is quiet and constant and willing to look upon the pain of the world with eyes of love. If Ace is his brother's superpower, it's not because he's superhuman. It's simply because he is open to the gentle faithfulness of mercy. He is willing to be a vessel of divine love.

Let mercy outweigh all else in you. The weight of mercy is a strange thing. It asks something of our fear. It asks us to enter into every relational moment with eyes to see beyond the surface of things. It means I'm invited to lean into August's refusal to do his homework from a more creative posture, a posture of love, of humility. I'm invited to release my top-down parental agenda and instead learn to be at rest, seeing his needs through a lens of compassion. When mercy outweighs the fear inside me, I recognize the truth of my son's struggle: this thing being asked of him is bigger than a simple assignment. The task is the small part of the reality we see. What's real is just beneath it—a little boy protecting himself from failure. *All the ways of the Lord—mercy and truth.*

My breath steadies. Brooks, sensing the calm that has finally settled around us, leaves his LEGOs in his room and walks the few steps into the hallway to sit on the wood floor beside me.

"Hey, Mama."

"Hey, babe."

"You okay?"

"Yeah, I'm okay."

"August!" he yells toward the door we sit in front of.

"What?"

"You okay too?"

August lets go of Ace, moving one hand to Ace's hand. He looks at Brooks. "Yeah."

I ruffle Brooks's hair and stand up. Ace still sits cross-legged in the middle of the bed beside his brother. I walk over and sit beside them both.

"I'm sorry I yelled," I say.

"I know."

"You know you're good at projects?"

"Maybe."

"You are. And you're good at fourth grade. That wasn't true what I said. You're gonna do just fine, just as soon as you move your tiny butt into the kitchen and start this project." I smile just enough for August to reflect it back. Always mirrors, he and I.

"I was wrong. I said mean things," I say. "Will you forgive me?"

"Yeah." Ace moves away from us both toward the end of the bed, where he finds a loose sock, perfect for swinging around.

"And August?"

"Yep."

"I want you to do your work when I ask you to."

"I know."

"I lose my temper because I worry you won't learn what you need to learn at school. It's not a good reason, but that's why."

August sniffs and moves his pillow to his lap, then notices Ace beginning to mouth his dirty sock. "Gross, Ace!" He moves to grab it from his brother's hand and looks back at me. "I'm sorry I yelled at you too. I really don't want to do that project."

"I know, buddy. I know."

* * *

It's a random Tuesday evening, when Ace is only nine or ten months old, when I spread a blanket out for him in the living room, place him on his belly, and hand him a couple of toys before stepping into the next room to salt the tilapia I plan to pan fry. The older boys wander back and forth between their rooms and the kitchen, asking for help or telling me stories. Every few minutes I peek around the corner to find Ace rolling on his blanket or reaching for the squeaky giraffe he likes to chew on.

Brooks has always been a kid with a song in his heart, someone who skips more than walks, a middle child living between two brothers who both, for very different reasons, need my attention and energy in ways that Brooks, due to his nature and his personality, hasn't required. He's a boy who learned early to please us, sing to himself in his room in the moments when August is struggling, build his LEGOs while I host a therapist for Ace. Sometimes I worry about the deepest stories he is learning to tell himself—that his job is to blend into the background and never demand too much. Who will he believe he is in the moments when he can't blend, when he can't please?

I hear his feet bound down the short hallway from his room to Ace's spot on the floor, hear him flop onto the carpet.

"Hi, baby."

Ace makes a sound in response.

"What ya playing with?" Brooks asks. "Oh, hi giraffe."

I pour a tablespoon of oil into the pan, watch it begin to bubble, listening to Brooks sing in the background. Then he stops.

"You know I love you?" he asks his brother. "You are a sweet little mercy." I walk toward the open space between the kitchen and the living room to peek at Brooks on his belly, his elbows propped on the blanket on either side of Ace's arms. Ace is on his back, staring back. Brooks puts his still-pudgy hands on his brother's cheeks.

"Just a sweet little mercy."

There's not a special blessing that Jesus gives to the merciful, except to say that the ones who give mercy also receive it. A cycle that begins with truth finding, naming the really real of our beloved goodness, in all our frailty, all our failure. That's what Jesus practices when he walks up that hill and truly *sees* the crowd of humans reeling from the suffering of their own lives. *You sweet little mercies*, I imagine him thinking.

The blessing of giving mercy is that it turns itself around. Mercy giving creates more mercy. And we who receive it somehow find the courage to give it back again.

We are all human and weak, struggling to love one another and longing for the world to be made right, learning to name the goodness we see when our eyes adjust to love. We are all those sweet mercies waiting to be blessed.

6

For the True Ones

Makarioi are the true ones. They will have eyes to see the Spirit of Truth.

It's a week before Christmas, and the children in our church are dressing up to perform in the lessons and carols service. Our church has two locations in San Francisco, and we've been attending the congregation in the Mission District, sharing space with the Spanish-speaking church that owns the building. They come in at noon on Sundays for their service, after we've cleaned up our doughnuts and cords and remnants of the wine and the bread.

At the church's other location, the children are in red dresses and button-downs and probably some sparkle for good measure, singing Christmas carols. I imagine they're a little more

119

put together, a little more practiced. But in our congregation, the children's ministry is a bit more ragtag. Our theme? An animal procession following the star of Bethlehem.

And Ace is the star.

My mom made Ace a star hat for the occasion and shipped it to us from Texas. Yellow felt, coated in gold glitter, with five star points that move out from his face in the center. The bigger kids, August and Brooks and their friends, a total of ten or fifteen children, have made their own donkey, sheep, and camel masks out of construction paper, felt, yarn, and Elmer's glue. Ace wears his star hat with delight, flapping his hands as we enter the back of the sanctuary and start walking down a side aisle toward the altar. I hold him in the air in front of my chest, Simba-style. At twenty months old, he doesn't yet walk. And he loves being up this high, especially as the eyes behind his little gray glasses recognize sixty or so pairs of eyes staring back. He giggles, and the kids crawling like donkeys behind us sing, along with the musicians up front, "O Come, O Come, Emmanuel." We make our way slowly toward the front, then walk along the stage until we reach the farthest side aisle, our animal friends mooing behind us along the wall of stained-glass windows. We arrive at the back of the middle aisle in time for the final verse, then walk straight forward, baaing and snorting accompanying us all the way.

As I hold Ace's body up, his star dust and glitter transfer to my hands, the carpet, and his red cardigan sweater. The moment captures something authentic within the story we're retelling. No pretense, nothing all that special to see here: some kids making animal noises, a collection of churchgoers giggling at the absurdity of the celebration, an off-key rendering of a classic Advent hymn. And a little boy who can't walk or speak but can hold his head up and flap his hands. He leads the room of kids to tell a story that feels familiar. The pure in heart leading the way for a group of shepherds and ordinary folks.

In the months before Ace was born, I had a sort of vision. Maybe it was mystical, maybe just the work of my own imagination. Who can say? I sat in my favorite spot on the couch, the side with the chaise lounge, my legs straight ahead, Ezra the cat curled in my lap. From that well-worn patch of couch, I could stare out the back glass door with a view of the gray wall of San Francisco fog and the barely visible Pacific Ocean a mile down the hill from our square rental house in the Sunset District. I spent a lot of time sitting there in those days, sometimes writing, sometimes praying or attempting to pray.

On that day, my belly taut but not yet swollen with the full girth of late pregnancy, the knowledge of my baby's diagnosis still ever-present, I closed my eyes. I saw a little boy, a child I knew was my then unseen baby. He was blond, wearing glasses, maybe eight years old, and walking up the big carpeted staircase at the church's other rented space on Sutter Street. The Russian Center's main room where we met for worship had—and still has—a disco ball in the middle and a Russian eagle crest above the stage, thick velour maroon curtains, and interconnecting chairs set out every Sunday morning. In my mind, I saw this boy walk on his own up the steps, from the entrance of the Russian Center toward the second floor, where folks gathered before the service for dough-nuts and coffee outside the doors of that disco-ball room. As this boy walked he was greeted, high-fived, *known*. This boy with a face so different from my own—almond-shaped eyes, thick upper lip, lower-set ears, soft cheeks—and at the same time a face like mine, with blue eyes, a wide smile, and blond hair. My son with Down syndrome.

I had experienced moments like this before in my life, those sacred glimpses, somewhere between dream and imagination, though I've never quite found words for them. My experiences of God showing up in an image of clarity or a sparkling experience of divine presence is hardly the stuff of scripture. I've never seen a burning bush or heard an audible voice, but I've felt a flash of love, a tender, hopeful knowing of God-with-me. And this moment seemed exactly that: God pressing in, hushing my fear, giving me an image of the baby inside me who I was terrified would not be known or loved. I watched my child walk up those stairs, high-fiving and smiling at the people around him, moving through the crowd with confidence—fully himself. And it was a holy gift. I opened my eyes and stared at the gray morning on the other side of the glass, the sun just beginning to press a small beam of light through the morning fog. My son would be loved, wanted, fully welcomed. Somehow, God had shown me.

I think of this nearly two years later as I hold up my child, the star of Bethlehem, his hands flapping to the rhythm of the Advent hymn. My son, behind in speech and in physical development, struggling to gain weight, whose vision will always be limited. My son, who will always be different, outside the norm of development, intelligence, and socialization: He is the star the whole room follows. He is the one leading us to Jesus.

OCTOBER 2022
NEW JERSEY

I've stopped my work to meet the school bus—one of my favorite moments of each day, when Ace's face arrives at the top of those three wide bus stairs. He grins today, a relief. When he's sad or angry, I often have no story to explain his feelings. Sometimes I find enough information in the daily report his aide sends home. But sometimes I don't. School is a part of his life I can hardly know. Today he smiles and side-eyes me. I know what he's getting at. "No, buddy. You need to walk down the stairs."

He takes one step, then sparkles those eyes again, prepping me to save his life. "Ace," I say with my sternest mom voice. "It's not a good idea to jump." But I hardly get the words out before he's squatting and leaping to me. My arms fly to catch him before I even finish the word *jump*. He's a thirty-nine-pound seven-year-old, and if I wasn't so worried about his individuation, I'd carry his tiny body everywhere he wants to go. I set him down on the street and grab his hand, waving off the bus driver. On the sidewalk I squat to look in his eyes. "Hey, it's not safe to jump off the bus stairs." Ace smiles. "I know it's fun," I say, "but you're getting big. What if I don't catch you?" He is unconcerned, though my squatting in front of him reminds him that he wants to feel my eyelashes. He lifts his hands to my eyes, his request that I blink against his skin. Ace loves all feelings on his palms, especially tickles. Since he was a baby in his crib, he's been lifting up his hands, palms forward, asking to be touched. Three years ago after a day at pre-school, I buckled Ace's body into his car seat as he reached his left palm to my right eye and felt my eyelashes brush his skin. He was mesmerized. Soon, his right hand reached toward my left eye as well. With both palms covering my eyes, I blinked my lashes against his skin. He laughed. He's never stopped asking for this.

We stay like this on the sidewalk in front of our house, his arms reaching toward my face, palms covering my eyes while I blink against his hands. Then I stand, hold my hand toward his, and we walk up to the porch and through the front door of our old Victorian.

We have a routine. I help him take off his backpack, and he hangs it on the lowest hook of the closet door. Then he sits on the stairs, where, with my hand over his, he and I remove his shoes.

"Put your shoes away," I say, the same way I remind him every afternoon. He stands from his seat, sneakers in hand, and walks three steps to the closet shelf, where we grabbed those shoes this morning. We've been working on this skill since school started, and he still beams every time he does it himself.

Later, after the bathroom and snack time, he takes my hand and guides me upstairs to the family room, where Chris has hung a stretchy, blue sensory swing. Ace usually swings on his belly, held by the fabric in the position of superman. He can swing in that thing from one side of the room to the other, which he does for as long as we'll push him. And when we decide we can't push anymore, he gathers the fabric just under his armpits and spins on the carpet like a Cirque du Soleil performer or takes a running jump and propels himself forward, gravity free.

Usually by this time the babysitter has arrived, and I've gone back to finish my last two hours of work for the day. But no sitter today. So I get into my favorite position under superman, lying on my back, so that every time his face flies past mine he giggles. And sometimes I manage to poke him right in the ribs with my tickle fingers, just enough so his laugh escapes.

"Blessed are the pure in heart," I typed into my computer at the dining room table earlier this afternoon after reading the notes I'd taken from the pile of books on the Beatitudes. The sticky notes on the table held words like *core*, *heart*, and *axis*. I'd written down, "It's important to understand that Christ never says, 'Blessed are the pure in mind' or 'Blessed are the brilliant in mind.'"[1] And I was taken with Frederick Dale Bruner's note that the Hebrew word for "heart" means "human center." Pure in heart, therefore, can be translated "clear at center."[2] This passage is not about action or desire. It's about essence, being, who we are all the way at the bottom of our very selves. Jesus calls that place inside us, where our deepest knowing lives, our heart.

Given our modern understanding of the brain and how our personalities and psychologies, emotions and memories, are all stored up in the big neuron-firing organ atop our heads, it's easy for us to think of the brain as the core of the self.[3] But when Jesus speaks to his listeners on the hill, he speaks to people who would have recognized the center of themselves as being smack dab in the middle of their chests. For most of history, the heart has been the place where we connect with others, where we feel and fall in love, where we ache and grieve, and where our personalities live—the truest parts of ourselves. What does it mean for that center to be solid, uncontaminated, clarified? It's wholehearted honesty.[4] It's a person who is the same in their core as they are in their actions, a person who doesn't need to hide any truth, whose center is exactly itself—real, all the way through.

Trappist monk, writer, and mystic Thomas Merton explained the spiritual journey as awakening to ourselves as we awaken to God.[5] What Jesus called the heart, Merton referred to as the true self, the person underneath all that seeks to hide it. Beneath our personalities, educations, talents, and egos, the self at the base of all our being can often appear as nothing.[6] But that nothingness, the self hidden in the depths of us, is actually our truest reality, the person we were always intended to be, created with love, fashioned by the creative force of God: "the face you had before you were born," as the Zen masters say.[7]

As Ace flies back and forth above me, the speaker blasting his current favorite, "Lean On Me" by the *Glee* cast, I come back to that Zen master phrase: "the face you had before you were born." This child, in his silence and stubborn insistence on holding his hands to my eyelashes or pressing the button on his talker ten times in a row when he requests dried mango every day at the same time. This child sailing above me, free from the burden of time or the weight of performance, has so much less distance to cover to awaken to himself as he awakens to God. It can sometimes feel like he was born there, existing in authenticity, while the rest of us spend our lives building exterior shells to protect our most vulnerable selves.

Those shells so often begin as necessary means to protect us from the cruelty of the world. But they can keep us from being known, from knowing and loving fully. Every identity we take on, every organization we lend our name to, every title and achievement we use to validate our worth, these are parts of us that never actually existed in the first place—all pretense, all smoke and mirrors. The image we create, the personality we shape over time, how we define ourselves and our own value are all an external coating shaped by our culture, our pursuit of approval, the quick comforts of pleasure.

But the true self is found in the mind and heart of God. And I wonder if that's what Jesus meant by "pure in heart." True all the way through, from skin and bone all the way down to our fleshy, beating center.

SEPTEMBER 2012
AUSTIN, TEXAS

For just ten months, Chris and I have lived with our two boys in Austin. We moved here with a three-month-old and a three-year-old, believing we were settling into a long-term home, a drive from my family, fifteen minutes from my best friend from college. And the year here has been sweet: Brooks has gone from sitting up the first week we showed up here to walking and, not long after, to climbing on a scooter, his face all thrill when it rolled down the driveway. Here we've danced in the living room, grown big, juicy tomatoes in the backyard, and made a practice of a Saturday treat at Donut 7. Here August played his first soccer game, in which he fought invisible dragons with slime, paying zero attention to the ball or his teammates. And every Sunday since the first week we showed up with a crying baby and a wild toddler, our church in Austin has been a safe, warm place for each of us.

Now though, Chris's company, which moved us here from San Francisco, has pivoted, informing us ten months in that his team is dissolving. He'll have a new role waiting back in the Bay Area. Suddenly, we're packing our stuff and saying goodbye to Donut 7, surprised that the life we've only just begun to build here will become a blip in the story of our family. The week before we leave, we're invited for the first—and last, I suppose—time to James and Kristen's house. James is the pastor of our church, but Kristen has had my heart since the first Sunday we visited and she followed me and my crying baby out of the service. "We love crying babies here," she said. Then she skipped the rest of the service, chatting with me while I nursed Brooks. At their house I'm delighted to find the walls of their kitchen covered with butcher-paper signs— poetry and quotes in Kristen's handwriting—her commitment to the literary indoctrination of her children via butcher paper is a life hack I'll copy from then on.

She's folding laundry on the floor while the four of us sit in their living room and chat. We tell them why we're leaving: the giant corporation's whim and our obligation to follow Chris's work back to our former city. As we talk, we all know our relationship is temporary. We may never see each other again. Our life back in San Francisco is established and more permanent than we realized when we left the city after only two years. Chris and I are buoyed by the reality that we have friends and a church community waiting for us in California. This hour in James and Kristin's living room is a chance to say thank you and goodbye. We chat about the details of our move. They ask about the kids, at home with a sitter. And then the conversation turns where I most love for conversations to turn: faith, Jesus, doubt. Kristen is holding a kid-sized T-shirt in one hand and pointing her finger into the air with the other: "If it's true," she says as she looks at me, "it has to be true all the way through."

She isn't talking about literal or historical evidence, not some concrete sign of proof. She means *us*. If this story is true in us, she's saying, if Jesus is true in us, then it has to be true all the way through our stories, our experiences, our way of being in the world. Our hearts.

I leave her house holding that moment and write it down, taken by its simplicity. *True all the way through.* What does it mean to give our lives to more than a spiritual idea? What does it mean for faith to coexist with doubt but not be squishy or easily shaken? I long for the Jesus story to settle so deep inside me that my internal way of being matches the teachings of Jesus that I claim—the humility, the pursuit of justice, the embrace of grief. In the years that follow, I'll think from time to time about Kristen's finger in the air—*all the way through*—and the kind of flourishing that comes from an ordinary, undivided faith, without pretense, without anything false.

FALL 2016

SAN FRANCISCO

Parker Palmer describes the spiritual life as a kind of downward pilgrimage through our interior darkness, a process of coming face-to-face with our false selves. It takes courage to "ride certain monsters all the way down, explore the shadows they create, and experience the transformation that can come."[8]

Ace is around eighteen months when he develops a rash on his chest. I generally take the laid-back approach to medical interventions. I use hand sanitizer after the park, but if my kid picks up a dust-covered Cheerio from our friend's kitchen floor and pops it in his mouth, I tend to giggle and say something about immunity building. Even though I've been diagnosed with an anxiety disorder, health concerns rarely keep me up at night. I've been a mom for eight years, and rashes happen. I hardly think about it for several days until Ace's checkup at the doctor, where I casually lift his shirt partway through my conversation with Dr. Goldstein about Ace's early intervention therapies and what milestones he's working toward.

"Oh," she says when I raise his shirt, going quiet as she presses the rash with her pointer finger. "When did you notice it?"

"Just a week or so ago," I say, my hand holding Ace's while he sits on the paper-covered examination table.

"You see this?" she says, touching her finger to the skin. "It doesn't blanch."

"Okay."

"A rash blanches when you push on it," she says. "When that doesn't happen, it's . . ." she pauses, gathering her words, "broken blood vessels. That's concerning."

I had been singing "Itsy Bitsy Spider" to keep Ace's eyes on me and distracted from the instruments she poked in his ears and shined in his eyes. Dr. Goldstein is my age and carries with her the kind of warmth I'm drawn to. We like each other. Though she's been August's and Brooks's pediatrician as well, Ace's birth has resulted in a constant flow of communication between us: referrals to specialists, questions, extra weight checks. When she shifts her face from Ace to me, I feel my muscles weaken, my breath catch. She's afraid.

Petechiae, she calls it. Broken blood vessels. A potential sign of blood cancer.

When I first received Ace's diagnosis and the brochure that came with it, "Down Syndrome: An Unexpected Diagnosis," I glanced through the long list of physical and medical concerns that occur more often in people with a third copy of the twenty-first chromosome. In those early days, the possible heart condition and of course the intellectual disability lit my fear. I'm sure my eyes skimmed the rest of the list, most likely as a defense mechanism to keep myself sane. I hardly registered the possibilities of sleep apnea, early onset Alzheimer's disease, the increased risk of celiac disease, autism spectrum disorder, seizures, and (there it was) childhood leukemia. The leukemia possibility became more real when Ace was six months old and we began our biannual blood tests, the ritual of checking his levels of red or white blood cells and platelets. When we go in to see Dr. Goldstein, it's been months since the last test.

I see it in her eyes: her fear for me, her genuine care for Ace. She keeps her voice steady and begins typing out an order for a blood test in the laptop opened on the counter next to us. She prints it out and puts it in my hand. The top of the order reads STAT. "You need to take him to the lab now, Micha." She levels her eyes at mine. "Don't wait."

I meet her gaze, my eyes filling, and suck in breath, willing myself to take the lab order from her hand. Ever a good student,

I open my mouth. "Leukemia," I say, looking back at the order, "is more prevalent in kids with Down syndrome." She nods. "Okay." I put the lab order in my bag and pull Ace's shirt back down. "Okay."

Dr. Goldstein watches me carefully, gathering her notepad and laptop. "Okay," she says, her hand touching Ace's arm before she moves toward the door. "We'll talk soon. I'll call when I get the results. I'm hurrying it through, so we'll know today. Okay?"

I nod, and she closes the door to the tiny, closet-sized pediatric examination room before my voice escapes from my belly—part sob, part yelp. I lean forward, laying my head beside Ace's body, forehead pressed hard into the thin paper that covers the exam table. A couple of breaths later, I muscle myself to standing, the tears hot and quick before I will them back. Nope, not right now. I stare back at Ace, sitting still, same spot. He gives me a smile, revealing several baby teeth, and I do my best to return it. "One more stop before we go home, buddy." I hoist him onto my hip and push open the door.

The lab is three blocks from the pediatrician's office, on the other side of the hospital where both Ace and Brooks were born. I buckle Ace in his stroller and walk, doing the only thing I know to do in moments of terror: worry, then pray, until the prayer drifts back to worry. In my fuzzy thoughts, I mentally flip back and forth between my longing to call Chris at work, begging him to fix my frantic heart, and the knowledge that I can and should protect him from worry. I will tell him soon enough, after this is over. I can do that. First blood tests. Then Chris. But maybe I should call him?

Lord Jesus Christ, Son of God.

My breaths pray for me, this prayer one of those most practiced and natural in my mind.

Have mercy on me, a sinner.

131

In and out I breathe, each step of my feet on the sidewalk keeping pace with the rhythm of the words in my mind.

Lord Jesus Christ.

I breathe out.

Have mercy on me.

I breathe in.

Lord Jesus Christ.

We cross California Street and walk west toward Maple.

Have mercy.

I *should* call Chris. *Lord Jesus Christ*, I pray. No. I'm not going to scare him. I can do this. Just a blood draw. I can do this.

Lord Jesus Christ. I cross another street, past Cherry, the street our car turned onto when we arrived at the hospital for Ace's birth, after I had labored at home with Chris and the doula for twelve hours. Right there in the ambulance entrance, I had climbed out of the car, my hands on the doula's arms, during one of the rare flashes of inner quiet between contractions.

I can do this. *Lord Jesus.* Ace and I take the ramp to the side of the medical building and walk through the front doors and straight ahead to the lab. I hand the lab order to the receptionist and telepathically beg her not to notice the STAT written on the top of the form, the medical lingo on the order. I beg the silence between us to stay. No acknowledging what I'm here for, no sad face of concern, no lingering of her eyes on the form of my baby in the stroller.

"Have a seat," she says, not even making eye contact. "We'll call you up soon." *Lord*, I pray. I push Ace toward the burnt-orange pleather chairs.

Back in 2013, I took a lay counseling course at church, a nine-month intensive in which I learned about reflective listening, understanding mental health disorders, and how the Enneagram can help us understand what motivates us. During one particular conversation about anxiety, Johnny, our teacher, explained how sometimes the only way to move through an anxious thought is to ride it all the way down. When we allow ourselves to stare down the possible outcomes, as awful as they may be, we invite our minds to move from the frantic fear and toward a different kind of knowing. There is a steadfast peace at the bottom of the worst-case scenario.

We're called back into the clinic's blood draw room, where for three minutes I hold Ace's tiny back against my chest and lift his arm toward the needle, singing in his ear as blood flows from vein to medical tube. And after his tears, his arm wrapped in a purple bandage, I push him back to the pediatrician's parking lot, buckle him in the car seat, and drive a short distance, crying, until my heaving breaths force me to pull over along one of the meadows in Golden Gate Park.

What if my baby has cancer? What if he dies? I think of Johnny's ideas about anxiety. What does it mean to ride a thought—the monster—all the way down to the very bottom, discover what is true under every other story we tell ourselves? Behind me in his car seat, Ace kicks the back of my seat as he stares at the trees and the afternoon dog walkers in the park. *Okay, God*, I think. *You want to go there?* I imagine the worst possible scenario, in which the phone rings and Dr. Goldstein gives the news she dreads. I imagine days caring for a toddler on chemo, his already-tiny body vomiting the poison, refusing to eat. I imagine a feeding tube placed right beside the chemo pump. I imagine long days at the hospital, coming home to Ace's older brothers, exhausted, nothing left to give them. I imagine the endless costs, the phone calls with the insurance. And his body. My baby's soft, tender body, weak in a bed, fading from me.

Down at the bottom of everything, what is true then?

I don't have an answer. But there, in the minivan, while Ace gazes out the window and nursery rhymes play over the car speaker, I go all the way down, my tears moving from frantic to heavy and deep. *Could you still be good?* I ask God. *Could you possibly still be good?* What kind of love can sustain a life, even when all physical evidence around says nothing can be sustained?

An hour or so later, Dr. Goldstein calls with the results. Negative. Later, the hematologist will pronounce his body mysterious, his rare bouts of petechiae a strange occurrence we'll experience several times a year going forward. Not cancer. Not dying.

That evening, I breastfeed him in the corner of my bedroom, its windows hazy with the orange sunset. I listen as Chris tucks August and Brooks into their beds, their giggles and wrestling noises echoing from the other side of the house. *Not cancer. Not cancer.* I sing one of the bedtime songs I've sung for all three of our boys when they were babies—my favorite hymn from childhood, sweet enough to pass as a lullaby, and something I rarely hear anymore since leaving my Southern Baptist roots. "All to Jesus I surrender," I learned to sing on Sunday nights when golden hour seeped through the stained-glass windows, illuminating my skin, glimmering off the light-brown hairs on my dad's forearms as we stood together in our regular pew, Mom up ahead of us, interpreting for the deaf congregation, her signs their own kind of music.

"All to him I freely give." I touch Ace's cheek, and his eyes flutter in the fading light of the September evening. What's at the bottom of surrender? When the very thing you're giving up is the one you're charged to protect at all costs? Underneath each dark monster on the ride down to the bottom of ourselves, what is safe? What is good?

"I surrender all," I sing, and Ace's lips slow. "I surrender all." His jaw relaxes and his lips part, partially releasing my breast. "All to thee my precious Savior."

That night, in my city, there are parents standing beside little ones in more than one pediatric oncology unit. They are living the kind of particularly cruel story that shakes a person, a family, to its core. I gently place my pinky in the corner of Ace's mouth, release the last bit of his suction on my breast, and carefully stand, the faded glow still enough light to see by. I carry his body to bed and stand over him, my elbows pressed into the wood of the crib's railing, and try to pray some sort of thank-you but struggle to even whisper it in my own mind. How do you thank God that your kid doesn't have cancer, that you don't yet have to learn the lesson of the pediatric cancer ward?

Ace's life is somehow scraping the edges of my fear, polishing me smooth. Before this child, I thought I knew how scary the world was. And now? What am I learning now?

Maybe believing in the kind of God that John the apostle describes as love itself requires relinquishing control, as if life is a delicate gemstone in your hand. If you close your fingers over it, keep it safe, you miss the sparkle of that stone, its bright glimmer. But an open hand risks vulnerability. Any gale force wind can knock that gemstone right out of your care. Is love really that? Open-hand, gemstone faith that threatens to scrape your heart bare, drag your insides down into the canyon of everything?

And what if I decide I want that sort of faith—the kind in which I open my hand and receive whatever wind will come? Mark Scandrette, author and teacher of Christian spirituality, paraphrases Romans 8 when he says, "Death cannot disrupt what is most essential to your well-being."[9] If the love of God is true, then it is true all the way through. All the way down to the bottom, where the monsters dwell. And I am true there as well, the me that originated in the heart and mind of God.

I pull the curtains shut, turn on the sound machine. Grab a Kleenex on my way out.

OCTOBER 2022
NEW JERSEY

When Jesus pronounces the true ones *makarioi*, the ones whose inner selves match their outer shells, he makes a promise: "They will see God." Later, at the end of his ministry, in his last act of teaching his disciples, Jesus will make another, similar promise. The Spirit of Truth will come to them: "He abides with you," Jesus says, "and he will be in you."[10]

Superman Ace flies over my head as the alto from the *Glee* soundtrack belts out "somebody to lean on lean on lean on oooooooon." The more I get to know this boy, the more I envy his way of living in the world, the ease with which he loves the ones who care for him, the simplicity of his joy. It's clear to me that what I held in my arms when I carried his Bethlehem-star body through the sanctuary and what I held when I lifted his arm to the phlebotomist are one and the same: they are an opportunity to take the dark ride down to my own truest self. Of all the statements Jesus makes in his Beatitudes, his promised ways to human flourishing, this one seems to be less a declaration and more an invitation: to return to the face we had before our birth so that we might learn to be true, all the way through.

"*Makarioi* are the true ones. They will have eyes to see the Spirit of Truth." The farther I move through this poem, the more the words circle through one another—truth, mercy, oneness, suffering, hunger, justice, and always back to truth. To see God is to see truth. To live this life of hungering for rightness, of living the way of mercy, is to know divine love that can only be pure: whole from the outside down to the dark bottom.

The true ones are the ones who flourish, knowing that the place we are most terrified to meet ourselves is actually where God is—holy presence, clarified light, at the bottom of everything.

7

For the Ones Who Serve Peace

Makarioi are the ones who serve peace. They will be
called kin, safe in God's chosen family.

Leah and I are both beyond pregnant by the time she and her husband, Jared, sit down for pasta at Locanda with Chris and me. *Ripe* seems like a better word. She is thirty-seven weeks; I'm thirty-five. This dinner was supposed to be fun, our yearly splurge at one of our favorite spots, the same restaurant where five years ago the four of us first met for dinner. It's a tradition we've carried on almost every year since. We've had this date on the calendar for a couple of months, enough time to find babysitters for their three kids, our two. Jared and Leah are among our closest friends.

She's the one I call last minute when I'm heading with the kids for a hike, when I'm desperate for someone to babysit in a pinch, when I need a good cry.

And Leah was the first friend in San Francisco I called with news of our baby's diagnosis, which hit both her and Jared particularly hard. They were told before we were that their baby showed a marker for Down syndrome. Their test was negative. And we all recognize that our story could just as easily have been theirs. In three weeks, Ace will be born. Jonah will arrive two days later.

"What do you guys need to know?" I don't have to ask how they're doing. Their faces look like mine and Chris's—sad, sleep deprived, confused. So many phone calls, coffee dates, and emails with frustrated and hurt people. For the past two weeks, our church has been in turmoil, and I've been at the center of it.

* * *

For years, my life had been beautifully intertwined with gay, lesbian, and bisexual friends—parents of my kids' classmates, neighbors, and coworshipers in a church where queer Christians had bravely shown up, despite their welcome being conditional. Our church liked to say we were open and loving toward the LGBTQ+ community of San Francisco while still holding an orthodox line. This meant we had a handful of congregants in our community in same-sex relationships, many who had made peace with our church's doctrine—and the stance of most Christian traditions, historically—that blessing LGBTQ+ sexual relationships would mean stepping outside the faithful interpretation of scripture. Our church held the line that while some people were naturally built with same-sex attraction in their design, it was sin to pursue sexual or romantic relationships. For years, queer folks in our congregation were asked to remain celibate in order to stay obedient to traditional biblical teaching. They could worship with us, but if they pursued a same-sex relationship, they couldn't join the church, couldn't be baptized.

For many in our church—and honestly, for me up to this point—this was the only faithful way to view same-sex attraction. The few passages in scripture that mention nonheteronormative sexual relationships seemed pretty clear at first reading, particularly Paul's brief lists of sexual immorality in three of his letters in the New Testament, what many in the LGBTQ+ Christian community refer to as the "clobber passages." It can be difficult for those who do not share my religious tradition to understand the significance the Bible plays in the communal and individual lives within the faith. In all religions, our holy books stitch our beliefs together. They explain the character of the divine, who we are, what we hope for, and of course our discernment of right and wrong in a world in which morality feels ever wavering. Looking in from outside Christianity, opposition to LGBTQ+ relationships can seem and sound like pure bigotry—and often it is. But it's also entwined with questions about how to interpret our holy book, how to faithfully structure family systems, and what sex is intended to be. Loving God wholly is intertwined with being faithful to scripture as we understand it, and we are warned that the act of rejecting or reinterpreting ideas from scripture may gamble the security of our faith—not to mention our family relationships and community relationships and perhaps even our own standing with God in this life and the next. The stakes are high, and the emotional and relational risks, both individual and communal, can be profound.

As I came to know my LGBTQ+ acquaintances and friends in the community and in my church, I also began to comprehend the weight of their stories of rejection inside their families of origin, their communities, and often the churches of their childhoods. Statistics show that LGBTQ+ youth are over five times more likely to experience suicidal ideation and self-harm than their heterosexual peers. They also experience more abuse, exploitation, and intimidation.[1] I had heard many stories of traumatized teens, who had been instructed by their spiritual guides or influenced by their community's response to queer identity and culture to repress their desires at all costs. When we ignore our longings, they eventually become our secrets. Most LGBTQ+ Christian youth of my generation were shown that secret keeping is the cost of following Jesus, the cost of preserving family support and religious safety. But secrets are like poison in the body. Poison eventually finds its way out, and it damages everything it touches. For the LGBTQ+ folks I had been privileged to know, much damage had been caused by exclusive church practices that pushed many of them outside the faith and sometimes outside the safety and care of loving family.

In my midthirties, I had come to a moment in my faith when I could no longer justify the use of scripture to teach exclusive practices while privileging my heteronormative life. I began to recognize that my faith tradition, my reading of a few New Testament passages, mattered less than the stories of LGBTQ+ people, their suffering, or their longing for spiritual safety and belonging. I had gotten this wrong.

In his letter to the Galatians, the apostle Paul explains how God's Spirit at work in the life of a person who follows Jesus produces good fruit—love, joy, peace, patience, kindness, goodness, faithfulness, gentleness, and self-control—often referred to as the fruit of the Spirit.[2] If a life or community that is rooted in the Spirit of God produces relationships and behaviors that are good, beautiful, and true, then how can the trauma and hatred heaped daily on vulnerable queer young people in the American church, resulting in mental health crises, addiction, and far too often suicide, be anything other than anti-Spirit? When it came to issues around LGBTQ+ inclusion, the fruit was rotten. Which meant the root, possibly even the seed of this particular tree, was not anchored in the life of the Holy Spirit. Love doesn't abuse, exclude, or mishandle the lives of God's beloveds.

"*Makarioi* are the ones who serve peace," Jesus says to the people, seventh in his list of Beatitudes. He lays out each blessing of his poem, each seeming to move toward the next, as though weakness, sorrow, powerlessness, mercy, a longing for justice, and trueness of heart are all movements on the way to this: peace, a way of living that transforms relationships, communities, and entire systems into wholeness.

When Jesus pronounces *makarios* on his followers, his blessing is not for those who are partial to peace, not those who hope for it, celebrate it, or even love the idea of it.[3] This blessing is for those who help create it, just as an architect draws the walls that eventually rise solid from the ground, or as an engineer calculates a well-made bridge, prepared to hold steady when the traffic comes. The *makarios* is for the designer, creator, builder—the makers—of peace. Or, as Franciscan sister Rosemary Lynch, a lifelong peace activist, explains, Jesus blesses those who live "in the service of peace."[4]

To become ones who serve peace, we have to move beyond hunger and thirst, that blessed longing for justice that Jesus describes in his fourth *makarios*. Serving peace is not simple. It requires that we put our longing into practice—empathy, dialogue, discomfort. Peacemaking requires awkward conversations, asking for humility and authentic generosity from both sides. But for all its messiness, for those willing to try, the practice of peace offers the kind of relational wholeness rarely found in our culture, where we are taught to avoid relational pain at all costs. Peacemaking cannot exist without intentionality, without generous embrace. To make peace is to cultivate depth in friendship, nourished by forgiveness, mercy, and hope.

. . .

In May 2014, I was elected to the elder board of the church Chris and I had joined in 2009, when we first moved to San Francisco. In deciding to accept my board nomination, I shared with my pastor that I no longer considered myself to hold a traditional view on LGBTQ+ relationships and that I was unsatisfied with our church's theological stance. My pastor, Fred, privately shared that he had come to the same conviction, that this would be a conversation the board would be having in the year to come. And so I signed on, with a sense of purpose and, if I'm honest, fear. For five months, our team read books, studied scripture, prayed individually and as a board, and wrestled with what it meant to be inclusive in the way of Jesus, particularly when it came to the valuable LGBTQ+ people in our congregation.

At the end of January, we voted to allow a noncelibate gay man to become a member of our church community, understanding that this decision, in an increasingly polarized theological context, would open the door to welcome all LGBTQ+ believers to become members and take on positions of leadership in our community.[5] We were blessing same-sex relationships. We were risking our own understanding of right and wrong. And we were reexamining what scripture ought to mean in our personal and collective lives. It felt like we were risking everything.

Where would we go from here? Pastor Fred laid out his truth to the board: in order to lead the church authentically, he believed he could no longer pastor a community in which LGBTQ+ believers were excluded from church membership and baptism. As we sat in silence around the table, I thought of Philip's encounter with the eunuch in the book of Acts. Philip faced a sacred choice when a man who would have been marginalized in his time for his sexual status, and seen by the religious authority as unclean, asked to be welcomed fully into the early church.[6] I wiped my eyes before we lifted our heads to continue the conversation. "What keeps me from being baptized?" the eunuch and the LGBTQ+ voices in my heart and life asked me. *Nothing*, I prayed. *Thank God, nothing.*

We would move forward with an idea, a middle way, in which we hoped to present our church with a new possibility: how each of us read and understood the few scripture passages around same-sex relationships did not have to divide our community. We could open our church to the full inclusion of our queer congregants and allow for everyone to wrestle with the passages in their own way. Our clergy and staff could be free to hold to either a traditional stance or a progressive stance on sexuality, believing that scripture gives us examples of believers worshiping together despite disagreement on nonessential beliefs.[7] How beautiful, I thought, if we as a church body find a way to live into this idea together. The board decided we'd begin this process gently, with book discussions and small-group conversations while also inviting LGBTQ+ people into full membership. This would be a difficult rollout, and the transition would be hard, both for the queer community and for those who held a traditional view. But wouldn't it be beautiful?

I felt electric, all nervous energy, joy, and apprehension as I drove home that night. I met Chris in the dim light of the kitchen at nine o'clock, my dinner of scrambled eggs waiting. "You did it," he said, bringing me into a hug. I laughed and teared up a little in his arms.

"This," I said, pulling back so I could look in his eyes, my hands on the sides of his waist, my pregnant middle pushing against his belly, "might be the most important thing I've ever done."

The truth is I had no idea what I'd done, or what I had left to do. Our decision was leaked via email to a large number of church lay leaders before we could announce it gently to the congregation. The anger, fear, and concern spread within days. The fallout was quick, and it was ugly. Many in the community, enraged by our decision, sent letters of exasperation, called staff and board members in shock and concern, and drafted group letters. As a board, we rushed to write a response.

Instead of a slow rollout, instead of conversations and book discussions, instead of time for staff and clergy to make peace with such a big shift, or even for individuals to make intellectual and spiritual space for a middle way, we drafted a letter stating our new position on membership for those who identified as LGBTQ+ and who didn't intend to remain celibate. Fred wrote a draft of the letter, and as resident professional writer, I combed through it, flagging awkward phrases, overly zealous certainties, and heady theological explanations. I added paragraphs and sent it back. He and I went back and forth over the course of a couple of weeks. When I finally approved it, I was sitting on the couch, my fully formed pregnant belly propped against the touch pad of my laptop. I cried when I gave it the go-ahead. "No turning back, no turning back," we used to sing in the Baptist Church. "I have decided to follow Jesus."

* * *

Two weeks later, by the time Chris, Jared, Leah, and I find ourselves at dinner, the letter has been shared on Twitter. Bloggers across the country have weighed in, conservative Christian magazines have slammed Fred and our elder board, and what feels like half our church has skipped out before any small-group conversations could even be scheduled. This is the loss Jared and Leah are holding. They've been part of our church community for more than a decade, since they moved to San Francisco after college. This shake-up has come out of nowhere, and our church, which had never been perfect but had always felt good to us, safe (safe, I've been reminding myself, only for those of us not asked to reject our sexuality), is on fire. And I feel like the one still holding the match. "Micha," Jared asks, "why didn't we know?"

I knew this would be an uncomfortable dinner, but I'd hoped the conversation might be about the experience of queer people in the church. I wanted us to talk about what it might mean to hold separate views on the interpretation of scripture or how I came to this place in my conviction, how the board made its decision. But for weeks, all the four of us have been able to do is frantically triage our bleeding community—the leak of our board's decision, the raging exits of what would eventually be more than 40 percent of our church members, and now our board's very public statement of LGBTQ+ affirmation, cowritten by me.

The conviction I held close but rarely shared, the decision I agonized over but kept confidential, is not only out in the open but also tearing our connections to one another right down the middle, rending the community into jagged halves. In all the hours Leah and I had spent together, we had talked about everything, but never this. I had been waiting for a time when we could have the conversation. That time hadn't come. "And you've felt this way for more than a year?" Leah asks. "You've been planning this?"

I fumble with the napkin in my lap. "Planning? No," I say. "But, yeah, for more than a year." I make wobbly eye contact across the table. "Months before Fred asked me to join the board, I had already changed what I believed. I told him. I said I needed him to know where I was, that I didn't want to lead if our LGBTQ+ policy stayed the same." I glance at Jared, then back at her. "I think I was afraid to tell you." She nods. Of all the things we've shared, this omission feels particularly painful.

"Though, of course, it feels like we've fumbled the whole thing. If I could go back just a couple of months," I say. "If I could try again . . ." I explain our board's plan to offer this change to the congregation softly, let the community come to an agreed-upon scriptural interpretation over time. And I share my frustration with myself for not having the wisdom to ask the questions that should have been asked. Was the congregation ready for this? Was the staff? And how could we have been so naive to think we could vote on this kind of massive change and then gently reveal its reality? "We made the decision and thought we'd work backward from there," I say. Jared sighs and leans back in his chair, his face all skepticism. "I know," I say. "It doesn't work that way."

"No, it doesn't," he says. I have always loved how Jared's emotions are never hidden. His joy is loud and encompassing. His sorrow, palpable. And his anger? Right now it lives in the molecules between us. "You know what people are saying, Micha?" I shake my head. I don't want to know, but I wait for it anyway. "That Fred stacked the board with young, weak leaders. That you all are afraid to say no to him. That you guys are puppets." His words sting. I feel tears prick my eyes. *Stop it*, I tell my tears. But they fall hot and fast anyway. I take one long gulp of air and wipe my face.

When I'm able to raise my face to Leah's, her eyes are on me—distant, gentle. I don't want to lose her, and I know she and I have always experienced our faith differently. We have needed each other's distinctions. I have wished to believe the way she does, reliable and unchanging. It's not that the world is black-and-white for her; it's that her faith is the steadiest part of her life: a solid mass she gets to hold inside her, carry in her middle and find substantial. My faith, while constant, is more mystery than mass, all vapor. I want to hold it in me, but it's always elusive, escaping my grasp. Our differences have buoyed our friendship until now. Her unwavering faith lifts my wobbly courage. My wondering faith has helped her expand her vision of God.

Perhaps Jared and Leah would have been better leaders for this moment in our church. I consider Jared's accusation. Am I a puppet? I don't think Fred intentionally stacked the board, but I do wonder if he was wrong to trust my wisdom. I wonder if, at thirty-five years old, I had the experience or gumption to hold my fifty-two-year-old pastor accountable. Maybe they're right. Maybe I'm one of his yes-people.

What if Jared or Leah had been in my place? Maybe they would have slowed the process down, spent more time thinking about repercussions. Or maybe, if they'd read the books I read, prayed as I prayed, asked for direction, they would be sitting in this exact place saying these same words. The truth is that my heart has transformed. I changed how I read the Bible. I changed what I believe it means to be faithful to God as a straight, married, cis woman. And I decided that to follow Jesus I have to open wide the doors to every human, regardless of sexual orientation or identity. I believe that my reading of scripture before this moment was wrong. It hurt people. And I can't lead any other way than this, no matter who leaves our church, no matter who misunderstands my faithfulness.

Later, I'll look at those rumors—the puppets, the weak leaders—and I'll see the truth. I wasn't weak. My fellow board members weren't weak. Facing pain, interrogating myself, and leaning into another's perspective are never weak. Was I naive, clumsy, frantic? Absolutely. Was I brave? Yes, I was brave.

"And what do you guys say? Do you think Micha is a puppet?" Chris asks, quick to protect me. I've been an emotional wreck, rushing to return emails and calls, then crying myself to sleep for the past two weeks. Chris is understandably worried about my health, the health of the baby. We don't have family in this city, and these two people across the table from us have played that role. They are a necessary part of our support system. I'm desperate for them to make space for my imperfections, to refuse to leave me, to cling to our friendship.

"Micha, we love you. We know you. We trust your convictions. But." Jared sighs. "It can be hard to stand up to power." He runs his hand through his hair and leans back, leaving his hand on the top of his head. "You didn't do this right. I'm all for having this conversation. I'm not for having it after the fact and only because it was leaked."

Leah tries to speak. She struggles to get her words out. And I know her. I know this pain between us isn't really about sexual relationships or God's design for marriage. I know Leah is generous, curious, and if we had time to talk more deeply, to listen to each other, she would understand how I've landed here, in a different way of interpreting a few hotly debated but small and nonessential passages of scripture.

This is about how I've led, my choice to participate in a vote taken before informing any leaders of the church outside the elder board, my naivete in believing we could contain any reaction outside our leadership circle, the hubris required for six elders and one senior pastor to—whether permissible or not by church policies—make this decision on behalf of an entire two-thousand-member congregation. The decision I made will transform how our church understands Paul's letters in the New Testament, how sexuality and marriage will be taught to the kids of our church community, and possibly even what our leadership will believe about what it means to be sexually faithful. Have I considered this? Yes, I have. I knew people would be upset, angry, distraught. And still, I hoped that most would feel the relief of this change, that their consciences would be like mine, finally freed from the twisted grip of holding a belief that felt more hurtful than life-giving, finally able to move from injustice toward joy and relief. I had hoped that despite the pain of these changes, our community, including these dear friends before me, would find a way to move forward.

"I'm trying to understand," Leah says and reaches for my hand across the table. "I'm trying to listen." Then she cries.

* * *

Those who are shaped by Jesus's words on the hill are invited to a new way of being community, a way in which their abuse at the hands of oppressors would never justify violence. In this new way of being—the way of flourishing—the community of Jesus is invited to practice honest dialogue, the freedom of forgiveness, and restoration of relationship.[8] Peacemaking to Jesus is not an abstraction, not a pleasant notion of a someday world. His poem and the sermon that comes after make it utterly clear: the life of wholeness—the really real of God's reign—begins with a different kind of community. And peacemaking is the heart of its practice.

There are no promises from Jesus in the Beatitudes or in his sermon that by loving our enemies they will be transformed into our friends, or that peacemaking will always create a world free of abuse or war.[9] But he does promise *makarios* to those brave and wise enough to serve peace, knowing that peace comes not through disengagement but only through generous confrontation. When Jesus gives his wild command to turn our other cheek toward an abuser after having just been struck, he is inviting us not to more abuse, as is often taught, but to turn our healthy and unharmed self toward the abuser, responding not from pain but from wholeness. This is the power of nonviolent resistance, because it demands that the accuser see the dignity of the abused.[10] And so making peace is demanding dignity through engagement, hard conversations, and deep wells of generosity.

The work of peacemaking among friends will always be a more straightforward and gentler path than the work of establishing peace where love has never existed. Perhaps our story is too simple to serve as an example. But, in this moment, Jared, Leah, Chris, and I are invited to respond to one another from our own wholeness, to work toward peace. It's not despite our differing convictions, but because of them, that we are invited to the really real. In the midst of our separate roles in a contentious community rift, Leah and I stretch our hands across the table. The work of serving peace together will be more demanding and intensive than one moment of honest conversation. Peacemaking is a spiritual practice that will require speaking truth over and over again, showing up to one another's homes when it hurts to do so, and holding one another's loss while embracing our own beliefs.

We begin to build peace by prioritizing wholeness in the relationships we hold dear, and then our invitation to peacemaking flows from core relationships out into society. No matter our level of connection or our gifts, each of us who follows Jesus is called to use our influence in the work of broader societal reconciliation. As long as there is racial and sexual discrimination in our communities, the continual threat of gun violence in our public spaces, and ongoing economic practices that—just as in Jesus's day—leave the poor more vulnerable to hunger, violence, and generational scarcity, we who follow the teachings of Jesus must see peace as a value we serve.

Living in the service of peace requires that we take our individual and communal work toward restorative justice seriously, even when the roots of injustice are deeper and stronger than our individual power. Peacemaking asks us to believe that our particular spaces of influence matter and invites us to hope that divine love can change systems, connections to one another, and even individual hearts. We can't seek peace and cling to righteous indignation at the same time.[11] To live in the service of peace is to see our own blind spots, to root ourselves in the kind of humility born out of love and truth. That's how we reject our own egos and hold to a rightness bigger than ourselves.[12]

Peacemaking never asks us to give up our convictions. At the Italian restaurant, Leah and Jared don't need to accept my newfound reading of Paul's letter to Timothy or my current interpretation of Romans 11 in order to love me. And I don't have to insist that I've made all my decisions with wisdom. But we're invited to a middle way, a way in which we continue to care for each other, to listen, and to dialogue through the differences between us.

• • •

A few days after our dinner with Jared and Leah, I am put on bed rest for my pregnancy, told to go straight home from my appointment to my couch and stay there until my little guy arrives. The baby's growth is slowing. His heart rate has become "concerning." And each biweekly nonstress test I've taken has resulted in my being told to drink more water in hopes that my amniotic fluid will magically increase.

Of course, on my way home, I pick up Brooks from preschool, knowing that if bed rest is necessary, it will have to start tomorrow, after I find someone else to take on these school pickup duties. I pull the car into the driveway and see a bouquet waiting at my front gate. With the flowers, I find a note from a writer on the East Coast, a gay Christian man I hardly know. He saw the board's letter on Twitter and got my address from a mutual friend. "Thank you," his card says, "for honoring me. Your courage is a gift." I can't even make it up the stairs to the front door. Brooks skips ahead while I stop, shut the gate behind us, and sit on the porch steps.

My courage? My courage feels like a dumpster fire most days. But here, pink roses and tulips, bright-green foliage in my lap, my pregnant body awkward on these concrete steps, I grasp that this might be the bravest thing I've ever done. And I'm proud. My church is imploding, and maybe I've fumbled the whole thing. But Jesus is here on these steps and here in this implosion, right where I followed him. Jesus is where he's always been, with his beloveds—the ignored, the beaten-up, the oppressed, the suicidal kid who hides his sexual identity or attractions for fear he will never be loved. "Jesus," I whisper, my eyes on the flowers, "thank you for letting me come here with you."

I wipe my face with my hands. Behind me, Brooks sings to himself, scribbling sidewalk chalk on the steps. I think of Jesus with his beloveds and remember that after his seventh blessing, his invitation to peacemaking, he makes a promise: those who make peace, who serve peace, will be called the children of God, chosen family. They will be kin.

In the LGBTQ+ community, both within and outside the church, it's not uncommon to find many who, having been rejected by their biological families because of their queerness, have instead found true and faithful belonging within chosen families.[13] Just as Jesus taught his followers that day on the Korazim Plateau, those who seek to be in the service of peace in the midst of rejection, misunderstanding, and even hate are given a gift. That gift is a new kind of kinship—in which unlikely or once-broken relationships can be transformed into unconditional care and belonging. Who better to teach us the way of chosen family in the dream of God than the ones who know rejection and have found family in spite of their suffering?

In John 20:23, when Jesus commissions the apostles and breathes the Holy Spirit upon them, he says, "If you forgive the sins of any, they are forgiven them."[14] Often the second part of this verse, "if you retain the sins of any, they are retained," has been misunderstood, though some, like scholar Sandra Marie Schneiders, interpret Jesus's words as inviting us to "hold fast" or "embrace the sins of any"—so that we can receive one another in love.[15] This interpretation invites Jesus's followers to do the work of forgiveness and genuine welcome. The service of peace that he blesses at the beginning of his ministry is the same one he returns to at the end, full circle. He instructs his apostles, in one of his last moments with them, that in receiving the Holy Spirit, they will find power to forgive and embrace one another.[16]

This is the kinship of peacemaking. It creates safety when the world feels dangerous. It guides the flower delivery, the dropping off of casseroles, and the decision to show up at the pregnant lady's house, toilet scrubber in hand, even when anger and rejection may be an acceptable response.[17] It's rarely easy to love another human, but the way of peace demands we make room to love in action, especially when there's pain between us. The service of peace asks that we seek to listen anyway, see one another in our need and brokenness and beauty, and choose to take care of each other through the ache of it all. Kinship is always both a gift and a way.

I wipe my eyes and smell the flowers. *God*, I pray—my hand where my amniotic fluid sits safe enough for another day—*I gave what I had. Can you just take it and make it something beautiful?*

FEBRUARY 2022
SAN FRANCISCO

Seven years later, I'm at Leah's birthday party, introduced by Jared to his friend, a pastor from another church in town. "I remember the first thing I ever learned about your church," the pastor says.

"I'm intrigued."

"It was that letter that came out in 2015, right after I moved here." Jared dramatically turns his head toward me, makes eye contact. I giggle.

"You know," Jared says, "around here we just call that 'The Letter.'"

"Yeah, well, it was quite a letter. I didn't agree with it—you know, theologically—but every pastor in this city read it."

"And all of Twitter, right, Micha?" I smile. That's right. "Micha knows something about that letter," Jared continues, his eyes twinkling. He takes a swig of his beer.

"Yep," I say. "I know some things." I smile. My acquaintance looks up expectantly. "I cowrote it. While on bed rest. Pregnant with a baby with Down syndrome."

Technically, the bed rest started a week later. But it makes the story ring. And I love a good party story. For Jared, Leah, Chris, and me, it doesn't matter. In the days and years that followed that letter, we experienced Ace's and Jonah's births, and Jared and Leah's decision to stay in our church community, believing that this one nonessential difference in scripture interpretation did not warrant leaving. We learned to lean into the beauty of peacemaking—seeing one another's stories, interrogating ourselves, and making room for genuine relationship. Jared eventually joined me on the elder board the next year, despite his more traditional stance on same-sex relationships. Leah and I planned Jonah and Ace's shared birthday parties, celebrated when Jonah crawled, then walked, and then celebrated again a year later when Ace met those milestones. There were chips and guacamole and laughter in their kitchen. And we experienced together the pain of watching our church struggle for years to come.

There at that party, Jared and I laugh hysterically the way only friends who have suffered together can laugh on the other side, the ache of that season stamped into our friendship. My new acquaintance stares in disbelief. "Well, that's not the story I expected," he says.

Peace is a slow-settling force, one that weaves itself between us in the moments that often feel most broken, most impossible. Like all the important things, it's hard to define and harder to notice when it's there, but it was the life force of Jesus's ministry and should continue to be as vital to those who claim his teaching. And it begins with authenticity as we practice, like Jesus, a kind of winsome, nonviolent invitation to relationship.[18] As we examine ourselves and admit our failures, inviting those who've hurt us to acknowledge theirs, we discover the beginning of unexpected siblingship, the assurance of Jesus that we will become the children of God.

It is how a church heals after it's ripped apart, and how a gay teenager who is told he doesn't belong, that his sin is irredeemable, finds wholeness. Peacemaking is the invitation for the straight Christian who finds herself in a dramatic church division, reconsidering long-held beliefs because of relationship, choosing to engage and wrestle with the experience of another. This is the way of flourishing. When we cannot find our way toward one another, we follow Jesus's example of listening, personal interrogation, and we lead from our own dignity and wholeness. We believe that change is possible, even when it costs us more than we think we can give. Peacemaking is never about winning. It's about humility and possibility, forgiveness and embrace, and in the way of Jesus, it's nonnegotiable.[19]

As Jesus promises, we find our unexpected kinship in the service of peace, a gift from the Spirit, who holds all our stories in one beautiful, hopeful truth. In the really real—despite broken trust, misplaced conviction, or angry rejection—peace is miraculously waiting in the possibility that family can always be chosen again, true repentance can actually transform hearts, and hate is never more powerful than love.

8

For the Ones Who
Suffer for Doing Good

*Makarioi are the ones who suffer for doing good. Their
dreams will become like God's dream.*

APRIL 2015
SAN FRANCISCO

The contractions start slow in the morning, only two weeks before he's due. My body seems to know that my mom is on an air-
plane heading my way to help with the older boys, and I'm grateful
both ladies—my body and my mom—happen to be on the same
page. Mom arrives at 9:00 p.m., and by midnight the contractions
are intense enough to call my doula, Jen.

I've never had a doula before, but I've never been more sure
that this birth must go a different way than the births of my older
babies. It feels primal in me. I know what I don't want—induction

via Pitocin with sixteen hours of zero pain relief, followed by the last-minute necessity of an epidural (first birth) or the heavy use of an epidural so as not to feel anything (second birth). I intend this baby to be my last, and though his diagnosis could lead to more health risks during labor, age and experience have revealed that there is more to the birthing of a child than the ordinary passage from within to without. There is something powerful, ancient, spiritual about the act of releasing a human into the world. And this time I want to be present for every moment of it.

Maybe Ace's diagnosis has planted a new-formed courage inside me. Maybe it's my age. Or practice. Doesn't matter. All I know is that this time I want to feel my body do this thing that medication tricked me into thinking I wasn't capable of before, the thing fear fogged me into believing I needed to avoid. It's the same longing I have when I sit beside a river, or hike trails, or stand on our deck and watch the fog roll in off the Pacific. My child will move from my very own body out into the expanse of everything. I want awe, and I'm resigned to the fact that awesome things can hurt us. The astonishing seems ever present beside the pain; sometimes it even feels like death.

In the days leading up to Ace's birth, in my quiet place where I'm forced to rest on my couch or in the bed, gazing out the window at the world, drinking endless cups of ice water, I take to wearing a T-shirt emblazoned with a lioness's face, ridiculous pink glitter blasting out from her eyes. I tell Chris I'm getting myself pumped for what must be done. But I think there's more to it. I imagine birthing my babe like that glitter lioness, alone in her patch of grassland, or like the laboring gray whale spinning in the sea until her baby escapes her. Maybe it's preposterous, asinine, to endure pain when relief is available. I've spent much of my life medicating every ache, every congestion or stomach bug.

But this seems different. I can't shake the feeling that the births I experienced with my older children only scraped the surface of my power. Since this baby's prenatal diagnosis, I've been forced to release his life, to reckon with the reality that his living will always carry with it a kind of ache. I can't explain it, but I long to feel this birth, exactly as it was meant to be felt. I don't know what will be on the other side, but my glitter lioness tells me I know this one thing: I can suffer for the one I love.

∗ ∗ ∗

Both the eighth and ninth blessings of Jesus's poem are devoted to a specific kind of suffering. In the eighth beatitude, Jesus blesses those who suffer for doing good. In the ninth, he blesses those who suffer for the sake of following him. In both cases, the suffering comes as a result of following Jesus's invitation into the reign of God, the way of prioritizing truth and goodness over power, popularity, or comfort. His poem of *makarioi* provides a "framework for understanding Jesus's own way of being in the world," and his justice-seeking, peace-serving, mercy-giving, grief-embracing way eventually ends in his death at the hands of Roman oppressors.[1]

The poem of Jesus crescendos to this point: weakness and grief, powerlessness and longing for justice, mercy, trueness of heart, and peacemaking all lead to persecution. Its theme is circular and muscular. We go around the cycle of the Beatitudes and find that in our grief and weakness, in our longing for justice and the making of peace, there is danger. Within the realm of danger, we encounter the nearness of God. And somehow, Jesus teaches, this results in flourishing.

My choice to give birth without any medication, without intervention, is not an example of persecution, but in the days that lead to my son's birth, glitter lioness staring at me in the mirror, I wonder about what draws us to suffer for the ones we love. Maybe I am trying to join my baby however I can, to tell him that I'm ready to leave the life I've had—the one in which I carried my able-bodied, easy existence along, refusing to see the power I held so easily.

• • •

The contractions are going strong by the time Jen arrives at 2:00 a.m., and I'm beyond grateful for her magical ability to lighten each one's intensity by pressing her fingers into pressure points along my lower back that I never knew existed. She's a dream. Jen shows Chris how to do her pressure point trick, and I joke that baby number three is a little late in the game for him to finally learn this particular witchcraft. After an hour or so, she sends Chris to sleep on the couch.

The contractions come hard and heavy every seven minutes for two hours during the night. And in between, Jen tells me to sleep. I do, dozing for five minutes at a time until each contraction rocks me awake in a wave of fire. She's there beside me each time. By 6:00 a.m., the contractions have begun to slow. She wakes Chris up. "Time to move, honey!" she says, handing me my coat. I put on my shoes and shuffle with Chris into the early morning light of an April-blue San Francisco sky. A good walk is Jen's prescription for accelerating labor. I hold my husband's arm and walk first to the giant hill two blocks from our house, where the water reservoir for our side of the city sits under a grassy spread. A few people are out doing tai chi at this early Saturday morning hour. There are some hard-core folks around here.

"You remember when we moved to North Beach?" I ask, reminding Chris of our first year in San Francisco when I was thirty

162

and he was twenty-nine and we lived in a tiny apartment with our one-year-old baby. "And all the little old men who did tai chi and ran in their jeans around Washington Square Park?"

He laughs. "They were cute." I take my arm out of his and wrap it around his waist, where his fleece jacket makes for an easy grasp. "You and August were both a mess then," he says.

"We were growing and learning!" I laugh. He's right. August roared into toddlerhood, and I cried after him. It took us both a while to get our bearings. I know we're still both working it out.

Chris looks around. "But living on this side of town has been good to us, huh?"

"Yeah," I say, taking in the fog still hovering in the sky over the ocean, a couple miles away. It rolls in three times as often as it did in the hipper, more expensive part of the city where we started out. We've ended up on the edges, where thirtysomethings move to have babies, where there's more space and fewer boutiques or around-the-block lines for loaves of artisan bread. Both are real San Francisco, but this side of the city has a less polished feel. And it's begun to feel like home, fog and all.

A contraction hits furious and hot, beginning in the middle of my body and shining out like I am the sun, lighting up the world, burning everything around me. Chris disappears. When I return, he's still there, his hands on my hips, my body bent at the waist, head against his chest. There are tears on my face. I wipe them.

"Hi," I say.

"Hey." He helps me stand up. "You got it?"

"Yeah." I wipe my face again. "Whoo!" I try to smile. "More fun to come."

Chris looks at me in a way I only see from time to time. When you live with someone you love and you have to pay bills, brush children's teeth, and argue over whose turn it is to load the dishwasher, it can be hard to look at each other and remember this thing—this magic. Not just the magic we found when we first fell in love, which, to be honest, felt especially easy, certain. I loved him and he loved me before we knew what to do with ourselves. But here—after two babies, one miscarriage, one terrifying prenatal diagnosis, and one brutal month of church and friendship upheaval—a new protective tenderness has grown between us. Here we are, about to bring another baby into the world, and everything will change: our family, our marriage, this entire season of our lives.

We're standing on the corner of Twenty-Eighth Avenue and Ortega. He takes my hand, and we cross the street. "We'll never be a family of four again, you know."

"Ugh, thank goodness. I was getting so tired of that," I say. He laughs. I love making this man laugh, even when I'm in the mid-stages of labor. "What will you miss?" I turn my head to look at him.

He meets my eyes, then looks back down to guide my elbow, careful to make sure I see the curb as we step over it. I roll my eyes. I may be in labor, but I haven't forgotten how to cross the street. "My wrestling matches with the two of them," he says. "The way I can hold each of my kids' hands in mine. The way you can read to one and I can read to the other."

"Yeah," I say. "Gonna be outnumbered." He nods his head.

"But also?" I look at him, waiting. "Also, I think it's just the reality that they'll never be babies again. I mean, this little guy will, and I can't wait. But August, Brooksie? We can't go back with them. That part's done now."

We walk two more blocks before the fire comes again and the world goes dark. "That was four minutes, babe."

I breathe, finding myself facing him, holding his arms. "Yeah, okay."

"I think we should walk back," Chris says as he turns us around and guides us past Safeway and the print shop on Noriega, all the way to our house, where Jen is waiting.

A few hours later, after we arrive at the same hospital where Brooks was born, my contractions are the only reality I know, a tunnel I enter alone, although there are moments when I look up from my labor to find other faces beside me. After my months of considering how I want to bring Ace into the world and learning that many women who give birth to a child with Down syndrome experience pity, sorrow, and "bad news" at the hands of their doctors and nurses in the delivery room, I come prepared. Jen takes the letter I wrote weeks before to the nurses' station: "The baby I'm carrying most likely has Down syndrome. We've already received a prenatal diagnosis. Please don't whisper around us. Please don't say you're sorry. We are celebrating his birth."

The rest is all thunder. I lean my torso over the bed, feet in hospital socks on the linoleum floor, nails dragging into the sheets. Chris is on my right side. He whispers and touches my arm or my hip; he counts and reminds me to breathe. "You got this, Boyett."

Jen helps me adjust my body into different positions. "Micha, I'm moving you to this ball." Or "Let's try squatting on this stool."

My memory will be hazy later, but a few moments will remain sharp and luminous. As my body moves to the end of transition, the most intense and final stage of labor, I am placed in the bed in an upright, seated position, my feet in the birthing stirrups from the movies. I try to push, but it's not the right angle. I don't have the words to say that, so I try to crawl off the bed, awkward lioness that I am. Jen steps in. "That's right. Micha, you're right. This isn't working for you, babe." I raise my head to look at her, all wild eyes and obedience. She commands the nurses to place what will be in my memory a metal chin-up bar above the bed, which—I suppose—they had on hand. (Later I'll learn it's called a squatting bar and it's plastic.) "Grab that bar, girl," Jen says. And in the ten seconds between my ninety-second-long contractions, Chris helps me squat on wobbly legs. I grab it.

The hands that for all of my childhood gymnastics competitions and nine-hour-a-week practices gripped and slid themselves around uneven bars—callouses there still, just waiting to be used—hold my body upright. My feet are on the bed beneath me, knees bent in the yoga position I've been holding every day for the past two weeks. My throat spews a sound I've never made before, the inferno in my body threatening to light the world on fire. Who forgets the jigsawing skin and the circular emergence of a head from the gutted center of you? "He's there," Jen says. Of course, I know. But I release the bar with my right hand, shaking fingers reaching between my legs to feel his fuzzy, goo-coated head, halfway into the world. One more push and there he is, alive. My legs threaten to topple me over, and Chris grabs my body to help me back against the propped-up hospital bed so I can see him—his body all white mucus and blood, light of the world.

* * *

I don't come to understand anything about persecution at the birth of my son. My experience is nothing but the suffering of every person who has ever given birth in the history of humanity. I don't endure anything new, nor do I come to a transcendent *knowing* simply because this particular birth is completed without the presence of pain medication.

But when Ace is placed into my arms, his small body, his near-perfectly circular head—the one I had just felt rending from my body—I receive a connection I don't have words for. I understand that I worked to bring him into this world lucid on purpose, a promise to him that though this world may never receive him, though he may never be given the power or voice he deserves, I will join him on the side of the powerless. I will suffer with him.

I don't yet know how to do this. Maybe I can't. Maybe I've lived in my world of ease and ability too long to ever be what he needs. But I take him in my arms, his face so clearly bearing the visual cues of Down syndrome—extra folded eyelids, flattened nose bridge, almond-shaped eyes slanted up, cheeks soft and sweetly round. Chris kisses my forehead and leans across my body to touch our child. "This little baby," he whispers in my ear, "has Down syndrome."

I giggle and wipe a tear. There's no wild weeping for either of us, only awe, acknowledgment. Here he is, God's dream coming true. Right here in my arms.

* * *

There's something about Ace's newborn body, his sack-of-flour snuggles—a result of low muscle tone—that causes him to fold around me in a way more tender and gentle than I experienced with my other newborns. I spend the next two weeks "practicing" breastfeeding with him, his weak facial muscles slowly gaining the strength to latch and swallow. I follow our nursing sessions with pumping, then the actual nourishing bottle, a process that takes three times as long as with a baby who "succeeds" in feeding right away. Once he and I finish the process, it's time to change his diaper and start again.

These early weeks begin to reveal a prickly burr at the base of my ribs that will grow over time, a relentless discontent, a longing to force Ace's value upon the world by increasing his productivity. His inability to latch on will last only two weeks, but it will always be followed by something else he struggles to achieve: the slow-motion process of learning to hold up his head, sit on his own, crawl, walk, kick a ball, and of course speak.

Most of the time, the gatekeepers of hustle culture are just fine if Ace's life and worth are placed in what has been predetermined as socially appropriate containers of his value: Worthy of pity? Sweet? Inspirational? Local news and Facebook will give those labels all the love. But when advocates speak of the dignity of all, worthy of full educational and financial support, worthy of job opportunities, expensive medical interventions, and prime real estate, or when people with intellectual disabilities are no longer "cute" and are simply adults, the keepers of hustle culture's boundaries get uncomfortable. In our kingdom of performance, the winners are determined by speed, skill level, and physical attraction. Expose the system for the lie that it is, and the gatekeepers shiver.

My discontent with Ace's slower developmental speed, which I know intellectually will always be part of his life, pokes at my insides. Over time, prayer, acceptance, and recognition of my own inherent worth will teach me to file down the sharp edges of that prickly discontent. I will build a softer, truer interior system: the wisdom of human dignity. And once that knowledge is born in me, my concept of what gives me or my son worth no longer needs to match my culture's. I will slowly be released from needing to prove my value through my own ability, appearance, or success. Human dignity beyond accomplishment[2] speaks to the way Jesus went about establishing his vision of God's dream. In beloved community, we don't earn our place at the table. And in the dream of God, transformative justice requires equity, rightness, and truth, none of which are earned.

In the show *Ted Lasso*, when Ted finally finds the courage to tell his friend and psychiatrist the existential pain he's been carrying all his adult life, she spouts this gem: "Ted, the truth will set you free, but first it will piss you off."[3] There's something about truth that carries power, and Jesus, who gave fame to the first half of those words, knew a thing or two about truth and freedom.

As Jesus invites his listeners to move toward the work of mercy and peacemaking, he comes to the end of his poem of *makarioi* knowing that the truth is going to enrage the powerful. Persecution means suffering because of truth, because when we follow the way of Jesus into rightness, goodness, and justice, we break free from the systems that have told us our worth is found in work that pays our bills, in the unspoken caste system we were born into, or in the number we make on a standardized test. Jesus gives his listeners permission to refuse any power structure other than the one of rightness and justice. And that truth, he says, will set them free.

This wholehearted way of truth telling always points to the lies that are bound to crumble. When lies crumble, it hurts the system, the community, and sometimes the individual who does the truth telling. Truth is never received without suffering. And Jesus needs his followers to understand that this will be part of the cycle too. This will be part of the really real. *Makarioi* are the ones who suffer for the sake of doing right, of loving justice, of living the truth. Their dreams will become like God's.

MARCH 2023
NEW JERSEY

Saturday morning I wake to Ace pulling his entire toy organizer of rainbow-colored bins to the floor. This is how he wakes us on days we try to sleep past 7:00 a.m. He's pretty generous about playing alone in his room, and he has never been one to whine.

169

He simply stays silent and destroys things. Chris moans and is out of bed before me, bless his heart. I hear him open Ace's bedroom door, which is right beside ours.

"Dude. Seriously?" I hear him say to our little boy. And then, "Good morning, buddy. Give me a kiss." I imagine Chris squatting his six-foot-four-inch frame down to meet Ace's three feet seven inches, their blue eyes level. There's some rumbling around while Chris surveys the damage. "Hey, guess what? Mama's still in bed!" Chris doesn't need to repeat himself. Snuggles in bed with me happen only on Saturdays, and Ace is an earnest and devoted snuggler. He runs into the room, jumps onto my covers, and wiggles his feet under the blanket, displacing Richmond the dog, who had been hoping for the same open spot.

"Well, hello, sir," I say to the little boy in mismatched pajamas, smiling with his head on the pillow beside me. I give him a look over. His lower lip is still split down the middle, as it has been for the past month. It does this every winter, and no matter what I do to moisturize his lip, it heals only when winter finally ends. His hair is growing out, and he'll need it cut soon. We shaved it in November, after he spent the fall twirling it around so intensely that he formed a bald spot. Months of buzzed hair seem to have nixed that particular stimming habit.

Ace has a few ways he tells us hello. Sometimes he says, "ha," his approximation of "hi." Sometimes he uses his talker if he's particularly focused and it's available. But mostly—and especially if he's in a good mood—he touches our faces while we name our parts. He likes to go in the order of "Head and Shoulders, Knees and Toes," particularly "eyes and ears and mouth and nose." He touches each one and giggles as I yell them out in my silly voice. He goes back to eyes, and I blink my lashes against his palms. "Eyes!" I yell, both of mine covered by his little hands.

I wonder if I have any right to explore the meaning of persecution—that powerful suffering Jesus says will be the result of following him in a world that does not want the truth of human weakness, that cannot bear to witness its exposed lies of a caste system that still exists, the reckless separation of humanity into categories of haves and have-nots. I am still learning to shake off the lies that have kept me obedient to the world's injustice. Most often, if we find that we haven't experienced much suffering in our lives for doing good, it's usually because we've been aligning ourselves with power, not with those who have been placed in the margins of society.[4] In my white skin, it's been easy, simpler even, to ignore my lack of suffering. I will never understand the microaggressions and subtle stereotyping that those who are Black, Indigenous, or People of Color encounter regularly in a world where unconscious bias most often goes unchecked. And I don't know what it is to be counted among the weak in an ableist culture. I can't imagine what my son experiences in his classrooms, where his value is still determined by what state assessments say he should be able to write, recite, or comprehend by this age.

I, who have always lived on the side of power, who have rarely suffered for pursuing truth and rightness, will always be invited by divine love to share in the dream of God. And that love compels us "to speak up, to act in the interests of those without power, to meet oppression with creative resistance,"[5] the kind of resistance that flows out of a wholehearted embrace of truth, especially truth that hurts the status quo. This is the life Jesus embodied. A new order, a way of being. A way that just might get us into "good trouble."[6]

I pull the covers over my head and play peekaboo, a game usually reserved for babies and toddlers. And I don't even consider that I'm playing it with a child who is almost eight. There are other moments when this reality will come to mind and I will ache for the developmental progress that Ace hasn't made. But most of the time, I get to parent him in the truth of my own love, in God's own love. Right now is one of them. No suffering here, snuggled with my little boy, playing peekaboo with my blanket.

"Boo!" I shout, and he giggles. Then he pulls the sheet above my face again. "Where is Mama?" I sing, waiting a moment. Then "Boo!" We keep at this for a while. Jesus said that when we embrace suffering for the sake of doing good, the kingdom of God becomes ours. The dream of God becomes our own dream. I can't say I know what it is to suffer for the sake of doing good. But I am learning that I have spent most of my life aligned with power, and I want to live here, where the eight-year-olds play peekaboo, where truth sets the both of us free, where the life of flourishing is waiting right beside the ache. Here in the dream of God, the dream that is becoming my own, I am loved and worthy, and nothing I can do will earn my value.

Ace reaches his palm to my eyelashes. Here in the dream of God, Ace is good and worthy. No matter who it pisses off. Or who it sets free.

9

For the Fearless Ones

Makarioi are the fearless ones, the rejected or pushed out. They will find joy on the edges, coworking with God, transforming the world in love.

APRIL 2017 (ACE, TWO YEARS OLD)
SAN FRANCISCO

I pull out the rainbow bunting I bought on Amazon for Brooks's birthday five years ago and string it across the living room and into the dining room and kitchen. Soon, our house in the Sunset District will be filled with friends of Ace and Jonah. Chris is blowing up balloons. The doorbell rings, and August runs to buzz Leah, Jared, and their four kids into the gate. He unlocks the front door and yells down the outside stairs.

"Happy birthday, Jonah!"

Jonah walks up the stairs at toddler speed, smiling and holding the hand of his biggest sister, Lyla. He sees August at the top and yells, "Happy birthday!" in response.

"No, buddy," August says. "It's *your* birthday. But you can say it to Ace too!"

Ace is in the living room on the floor crawling after balloons as fast as Chris blows them up. Even if only Jonah's family arrived for the party, with Jared's giant voice and the energy of their four kids running through the house with ours, it would be loud enough to feel like a party. But soon guests begin to arrive. There's Ace's playgroup of four other toddlers in the city with Down syndrome, as well as another little boy with Down syndrome who lives an hour south in Palo Alto. Jonah has invited a couple of neighbors. And, together, the boys have a crew of shared friends from church. Soon our house starts to feel like one of those dancing houses in cartoons, jiggling from side to side on an otherwise still block.

Ace's playdate and therapy friends gather on the floor in the kitchen, where a few parents rain balloons on their heads. I could spend the rest of this party watching their perfect, upturned faces waiting for the balloons to make contact, but Brooks and his buddies Johnny and Levi run out of the kitchen holding handfuls of chips, and I have ideas of what they might do with those crumbs in the back bedroom. I follow them and manage to turn their train around and send it toward the open back door.

I love looking around the room. It's really too small here for the number of people. And though I can easily get overwhelmed, seeing these faces—of close friends whose kids I know well and of those in the Down syndrome community who we are only just beginning to connect with, all chatting across the couch or the chairs that have been set around the room, balloons lifting and falling around them—fills me up. The doors open out to the gorgeous, blue-skyed April day, where folks have gathered on the deck. There is so much life here.

When we circle around Ace and Jonah at the toddler table my parents gifted Ace for this particular birthday, Ace and Jonah sit side by side. Neither of them knows how to blow out his candles. Ace's flicker out all on their own while Chris holds back his curious hands, which really want to touch the flames. After the song, Jonah tries his best to blow but eventually needs help from his older brother. Both boys equally appreciate their chocolate cake. There's no developmental difference in loving chocolate. Some things are innate.

After the party, a few families stay behind to help clean up. It's afternoon, and after cleaning we walk to the park a few blocks away. Ace isn't walking yet, but for the past month he has been on his feet, using a toddler-sized, hospital-grade metal walker that opens in the front. It's taken him a while to get the hang of it, but he has figured out how to keep his hands on the red handles and propel his feet—mostly—in a forward direction. He still tends to veer into curbs, trees, fences, flowers, and toys. Walking beside him and his walker demands constant vigilance.

At the playground, their friend Joshua zooms around on a tricycle, while Jonah takes to directing Ace's walker. He holds the back metal rod of Ace's walker, pushing him a little too fast down a small hill, past the garden, and onto the squishy new padding of the playground. Soon I'm chasing them both as Jonah directs Ace and his walker under the wild and dangling feet of kids on the monkey bars. Ace's feet, like those of a Looney Tunes character, struggle to keep up with Jonah's speed and the rest of his body.

"Jonah!" I run behind him, touching his back and getting my hand onto Ace's walker. "Sweetie, I think you're pushing a little faster than Ace can walk."

"Okay," Jonah says.

175

"Just let him walk himself, and you can help him not run into other kids and toys, okay?"

Jonah nods his head, and the pair of trouble turns to move toward the swings. I make eye contact with Leah across the park, and we laugh. Then I run after them in time to prevent them both from getting their beautiful heads slammed by propelling feet. I love these two boys together and Jonah's insistence that Ace needs to be directed around this space. Toddler leading toddler. Ace's legs are still weak, even after a month moving in this position, standing on their own, held up under the sturdiness of this metal cage on wheels around him. Jonah just popped up on his feet one day, the same as my older boys did. The human body is remarkable, both in its ease and in how difficult any small difference in development, low muscle tone in Ace's case, can make a task. I'm amazed by Jonah's intuitive understanding that Ace is not broken, just a bit more fragile than he is, in need of his direction. No pity here, only necessary brother love: friendship.

Ace, you walk. I'll drive from behind.

* * *

It occurs to me as I watch this pair of two-year-olds that both of them—the one who struggles to place his feet, holding to his tiny metal walker, and the taller, stronger little boy behind him, navigating his friend in circles, even while every swing and slide, climbing structure, and potential playmate is available to him— are learning to exist together. They are learning how to be in beloved community.

Jonah has everything going for him: a handsome white boy growing up in a thriving city, son of two parents with college degrees and good careers. In the world as it is right now, Jonah is set up to be among the privileged few, among those to whom all ease and opportunity will be available. As he grows, he will have the option to live so comforted by his own experience of life that he may miss seeing his circumstances for what they are: inequitable. He could miss the reality that most people in the world will know a less generous, less comfortable, less safe experience of the world than what he has known. He can choose to ignore the struggles of those who live daily in a society in which unwritten rules of caste have kept them from having access to the education, nutrition, or social safety that will be available to him.[1] But because of love, because of community, Jonah has been and is being invited into a new order of the world, and this is the kind of invitation that just may settle so deeply in his body that he will never be content to live the easy life while others struggle. He straightens Ace's walker again, this time away from the swing set and the feet dangling from the climbing structure, and they start fast-walking toward the baby toys.

Jonah, I realize, in his love for Ace, is like all of us who are invited—whether through relationship or through our own suffering—to join the dream of God that Jesus speaks of on the hill. "Blessed are you," Jesus says as he closes his strange poem, "when people insult you and persecute you, and falsely say all kinds of evil against you because of Me. Rejoice and be glad, for your reward in heaven is great; for in this same way they persecuted the prophets who were before you."[2] Often we think of persecution as harm being done against us: being imprisoned for our beliefs, being rejected for work or fair pay because of a deeply held conviction, losing opportunities because we won't bend our morals to get ahead. But what if persecution is weightier than the act of being rejected based on principle? If what Gregory Boyle says is true, that the Beatitudes are less a spirituality and more a geography, what if the rejection of persecution arrives more fully because of where we stand and whom we stand with?[3]

Those who sat and listened to Jesus's teaching on the Korazim Plateau may not yet have understood the kind of opposition and resistance they would face if they chose to adopt his principles for living. But we don't have to read far in the gospel stories to see how Jesus repeatedly invites his followers to stand beside the rejected, the misunderstood, and the exploited of society with transformative love. His invitation to embrace the ones on the margin is also an invitation to danger. *Makarios*, the gift of human flourishing, always requires love. And radical love often challenges the status quo. The more we live Jesus's radical way, the more we "speak and act in solidarity with those who suffer on the margins,"[4] the more likely we are also to be marginalized. Mark Scandrette calls it "the way of radical love,"[5] because following Jesus in solidarity with those who suffer requires a kind of courage. The way of radical love takes us where no one is forcing us to go, for the sake of Jesus.

"The earliest followers of Jesus understood that pursuing his radical way would inevitably lead to resistance and difficulty."[6] For Jesus, that resistance eventually led to his execution at the hands of the Roman government. Many of his apostles walked a similar path. I wonder if the early followers who suffered for standing with the ones their culture told them to ignore remembered their teacher's poem that day on the hill outside Galilee in their moments of affliction: *makarios*, the upside-down notion that a life worth living is one that aligns with the transformative dream of God, the remarkable vision of beloved community, a life that was never promised to be easy but that, through the way of Jesus, is making all of us whole.

In living the way of radical love, those of us who follow Jesus are carried through the transformative postures of the Beatitudes.[7]

On the margins, we learn to long for restorative justice and be-come builders of peace. We learn to see the world through the eyes of those who are often discarded by society—the disabled and the ones rejected because of their gender, sexual identity or orientation, race, ethnicity, class, or ability—the beloved of God.

We who follow Jesus may never transform the whole story of the world into one in which all justice is restorative and all people have access to health, community, and joy. But we can follow Jesus toward that end, living with the hope that all things will be made new.[8] And we can begin where we are, in our com-munities, when those of us who have access to ease, comfort, and opportunity choose to build community among those for whom suffering has been a close companion. We all need radical courage to build the kind of community where society's opinion matters far less than our own fearlessness, than our integration of truth within ourselves and our relationships. And as we do, whether or not that work brings us to resistance and difficulty, we can be assured that radical love will always lead to transformative wholeness.

FALL 2019
SAN FRANCISCO

"We talked about the ocean and played a game with a crab and a fish and an octopus!" Jonah is explaining to Ace and me as we drive back down Sunset Boulevard after picking Jonah up from school. He gets out of preschool later than Ace, and today he's coming over to play.

"Ace!" Jonah says, leaning his four-year-old body forward from his car seat to catch Ace's eye. "Hey, Ace!"

Ace doesn't reciprocate. He's focused on the sock he's pulled off his foot. He's dangling it.

"Ace! I want to say something to you, and you're not looking at me!"

"Jonah, honey," I interject from the driver's seat. "Remember what we've talked about. Sometimes it's hard for Ace to pay attention because he doesn't just have Down syndrome. He's also autistic, and it's gotten harder for him to look in his friends' eyes."

This statement is still one I struggle to say. The diagnosis of autism spectrum disorder is only two months old, and it came after a year of what the doctors and therapists and teachers all called "regression." Any progress Ace made in communication, sleep, social engagement, and academic skills as a two- to three-year-old began to fade so slowly between ages three and four that it took me nine months to notice. Jonah has grasped that Ace now hardly smiles at him when they're together, and I see the ache that causes.

"Ace." Jonah changes tactics. "I think you need to talk."

I look at Jonah in the rearview mirror. This dear boy who loves my son. I know what it is to long for Ace's success, to dream that he might be able to say the things he feels, to play the games he wants to play, to show the ones he loves that he is there with them, loving them back.

"Ace!" Jonah says, inspired by Ace's spinning sock. "Say, 'Sock!' okay? 'Sock!' 'Sock!'"

Ace doesn't reply.

"'Sock!' Ace, 'sock!'"

"Jonah, babe, you know it's really hard for Ace to talk." My voice catches when I say it. "You're a good friend. And it's nice of you to practice with Ace, but maybe we can find some other ways to practice."

"No, I want him to say, 'Sock,'" he says, getting agitated. "Ace, say, 'Sock!'"

There are times I can state all of Ace's challenges in one long chain of facts. With a steady voice in the doctor's office, I can list each of my son's limitations with a resilience and pragmatic fortitude only time has built. But right now I hear Jonah's need for his friend, and I feel it too—this desperate love, this longing for Ace to experience the world the way we do, this desire that he suddenly say what we know he wants to say, that we might get a hint of the deepest parts of him, the mind we love but can't fully know.

"Jonah, honey."

"I know," Jonah says, "because he has Down sin drum."

"Yeah," I say and pause, then decide to continue. "But, Jonah, a lot of kids with Down syndrome can talk, even though Ace can't talk yet." Tears gather in my eyes. "And that makes me sad." I wipe my face and raise my eyes to the rearview mirror. "I wonder if that makes you sad too."

. . .

It can appear that Jesus simply repeats himself when he gives this final *makarios*. In fact, for much of Christian history, many have suggested that Jesus gave only eight beatitudes and that the last two are so similar in nature that they ought to be considered a combination blessing, just a little longer than the rest. But many modern theologians believe Jesus intended there to be nine points to his structure of *makarioi* and that his final two blessings work off each other to emphasize the reality of persecution his followers would face. Theologian Jonathan Pennington calls it a kind of "add-on, bonus feature" that places "great stress and weight on the theme of persecution by making it the repeated and climactic note."[9] These final two beatitudes emphasize how unexpected this list actually is. Who promises flourishing in the midst of suffering?

This kind of persecution will come not from who Jesus's followers are but from what they choose to do, as Jesus emphasizes in both the eighth and ninth beatitudes. While most of the earlier beatitudes are universal, the final two are particularly for his followers. They are invited to a radical new way of living in the world. And this way will require all their courage, because the life of flourishing is one in which meaning surpasses safety, in which the joy of loving community exceeds the instinctive protection of ourselves.

The promised way of Jesus is still available to us now. We live in an especially anxious time. Though our technology promises to make us more comfortable and connected, it often just stokes our fear, increasing loneliness, separating us from the dependent goodness of community. Jesus's macarisms can become a "powerful antidote to the contrived happiness of consumerism and mindless entertainment of our day."[10] In other words, Jesus's final beatitude isn't just an invitation to be persecuted for following his path. It's an invitation to live outside our natural state of fear, an invitation to courage within community.

Fear can contain us in our "small, separated self," keeping us from the fullness of reality.[11] The way of beloved community then becomes the way of persecution and also the way of the pureness of heart and integrity. When we live outside our small, false selves and reach into the spaces of marginalization around us, we enter the cyclical story of Jesus's *makarioi*. When we join those on the margins in their place of suffering, we become poor in spirit. We grieve. Our eyes are open to injustice, and we hunger and thirst for the world to be made right. We work in the service of peace. We live "discontented with the present reality."[12] And so, we begin the circular pattern of Jesus's poem all over again.[13] These *makarioi* statements can never be pitted against one another.[14] Instead, they flow. The ninth beatitude works to summarize all the beatitudes, pointing us again to the limits and longing that draw us back to our own poverty of spirit, and therefore back to the grace of Jesus.[15]

While in the eighth beatitude Jesus explains that his followers will experience persecution for the sake of righteousness—rightness and justice—he expands his understanding of persecution's cause in the ninth. By the time he repeats his call to suffer, he is inviting his followers to endure affliction for the sake of following *him*, understanding that the way of rightness and justice will always be the way of Jesus.[16] The way of Jesus will result in joining our lives with the ones who are already suffering. This is the cycle of the poem Jesus sets before the ones who have come to hear him preach.

Maybe that circular pattern is why Jesus doesn't tidy up his final *makarios* in the same way we see him do in the other blessings. While the other *makarioi* conclude the "blessings upon these sorts of people" with a "for they will" statement that names their relationship to God,[17] his final statement is longer, lingering: "Find joy," is Jesus's message to us, because you are joining the great ones—the prophets, the rejected, coworkers in the dream of God. Together, we will transform the world in love.

The final *makarios* of Jesus is a call to courage. This is the whole and flourishing life, he says. The world may beat us up and cast us out, but following Jesus is a gravitational pull into the cycle of the dream of God, where, as Stephanie Spellers says, "God, whose very nature is love and who has created a world and sustains the world . . . is transforming the world in love."[18]

The Beatitudes invite us into the ache of this purpose and calling: to embody the deep-down truth of our poverty of spirit, our grief, our powerlessness, our longing, the mercy we have available, the integrity of our hearts, the peace we make, and our willingness to enter into suffering with the ones who suffer. This is the narrative that teaches us to live fearlessly, integrating our joy and our pain, becoming our realest selves. We are being restored to wholeness as we restore the world around us to wholeness.

SUMMER 2021
NEW JERSEY

It's been a year since we moved in the middle of the COVID-19 pandemic. Ace's diagnosis of autism spectrum disorder came only a few months before the CDC's lockdown orders. But both revealed that I no longer had the energy and sheer willpower to give my little boy every intervention he needed to thrive, every therapy the school district was too financially strapped to provide. Before the pandemic hit, we were looking for jobs on the other side of the country, closer to Chris's family, or closer to mine, in states with more funding to provide Ace with the intervention he needed.

Months of virtual school appeared to be rolling into another year of virtual school, a challenge for all kids but especially for kids like Ace, who need extensive sensory input, creative visual cues, and interaction with peers and adults in order to learn. I feared that after Ace had lost so many skills over the past year and a half, more months of forced virtual education would take even more from him. So Ace became our family's priority in that wild and uncertain season of social upheaval. If, after more than a decade in San Francisco, we were going to move to a place that could afford to give him the education he was rightfully promised, we needed to do it then. So in August 2020, five months after lockdown began, we bought a house in northern New Jersey, packed our life into boxes, and carefully flew mid-pandemic across the continent to start again.

I had worried when we left that Jonah would forget about his love for Ace, this friend of his heart who shared his birthday, whom he lay beside as a newborn, pushed via walker through the park, and eventually jumped beside for hours on various trampolines. But one year later, during his family's summer visit to our blue house in New Jersey, Ace stands for breakfast— creature of habit that he is—on his favorite wooden stool we call a "tower" for its walls that rise around him to his armpits, and Jonah squeezes himself into the tower as well. The boys shoulder to shoulder, Jonah carries on enough conversation for the two of them.

"Your pancakes look good! You like a lot of syrup, huh? I hope we get to go swimming today. Remember yesterday when your dad made that giant splash and you laughed so hard? Hey, Ace, I'm going to have a bagel. Papa, can I have a bagel? Ace!" Ace turns to look at Jonah. He has made a lot of progress with turning his head to face his friends when they talk to him. "Have you ever done a cannonball into the water?" Jonah thinks for a beat. "No, you probably haven't because Mom says you can almost swim on your own, but not quite yet. But next year you will. And when you do, you should learn to do a cannonball and we'll splash each other and we can measure how tall our splashes are, okay?"

Jonah's bagel is ready. Jared slides it onto the counter next to Ace's peanut butter pancake. The two boys clad in summer pj's eat side by side, one an entire neck and chest taller than the other. "Thanks, Papa."

That night, after the big kids' and Jonah's competition for splashiest cannonball and Ace's individual and artful plunging in the shallow end, our combined seven kids play so late in the yard that the sky turns slate blue, their voices rising and carrying, the way only the voices of children can do. Mid-August and we can feel the summer's endless days sneaking away from us. Tomorrow Leah, Jared, and their four kids will hop on a plane and soar west to California, where school has already begun. We still have three weeks before we go back. The mosquitoes seem as anxious as we are to grab the last bit of summer. Jonah, Ace, Leah, and I walk out in front of the houses on our block and stroll in the dusk down the sidewalk, Jonah holding Richmond the dog's leash.

Ace has giggled all night, the constant noise and excitement of four extra kids in our home enough of a buzz to keep him going long past his bedtime, but just as we get to the end of the block, exhaustion hits him. He plops to the sidewalk on his bottom, unwilling to stand and move his body the rest of the way down the street.

"Oh, buddy," I say, "you're right. It's way past time for bed." I am just about to step in and pick Ace up when Jonah interjects.

"Ace! You're so tired! Don't worry, bud. I got you. I got you." He leans over and begins to shift Ace's body. Ace, recognizing that his friend is going to do the heavy lifting and not his mom, decides to help out a bit and moves onto his feet just enough to give Jonah a little room to lift.

Jonah makes a grunt and then hoists Ace's body, three-fourths the size of his own, into his arms. He dangles him all the way home, one little boy carrying another along the sidewalk in the dark, coworkers in the dream of God.

EPILOGUE

For the Lights of the World

Two days after Ace's birthday, I wait outside the terminal at the San Francisco airport, keeping watch for Leah's dark-gray minivan. She smiles wide, waving as she pulls up. The last time I was here, nine months ago, they had just gotten a new puppy. Now he's full-grown, greeting me in the van's second row, tail beating the empty bucket seats, where we used to buckle in our babies for adventures.

I'm here for a speaking engagement, and I'll be renting a car and driving out to a retreat center in the morning. But I came a day early—Jonah's birthday. Leah really doesn't have time to be picking me up at the airport. Her family has recently lost a loved one, and their weekend will be focused on extended family and the memorial service. But there is still enough time to celebrate Jonah, who arrives home from school an hour before his older siblings, his hair shaved on the sides with a rattail mullet, one of those haircuts only an eight-year-old with parents who believe

187

in the importance of autonomy and self-expression would have. He looks awesome.

He has a gift card to the local sporting goods store, and he, Leah, and I spend the hour scouring the aisles for the perfect sneakers. He gives up and buys two lacrosse sticks and a ball. Back at the house, I bake his birthday cake while Leah makes dinner, my presence in their home like the old days, except without the kids I would have brought along with me. I ache for the chaos.

Once the cake is in the oven, Jonah asks to see what I gave Ace for his birthday, a fabric outdoor zip line we stretched from one tree in our New Jersey backyard to the other. I pull out my phone to show him a video of Ace giggling and holding his feet in the air as he sails through the sky, a foot and a half above the ground. Then Jonah grabs some paper and markers, and I watch him begin to make a card, crafting with scratchy handwriting a note for my son. Black block letters and balloons: Happy Birthday, Ace! Your friend, Jonah.

During the next two days, I will speak to a crew of middle and high school students I know from my time in San Francisco. I'll show them a picture of the Korazim Plateau and tell them some say Jesus preached his most famous sermon here. I'll ask, "Who is Jesus?" and then I'll show some of my favorite cringey Jesus memes from the internet: Jesus on a cross-shaped skateboard, Jesus poking his head out from around a corner, Jesus taking a mirror selfie.

"Jesus," I'll say, "shows us how to understand who God is. And how to understand who we are."

It's not much more complicated than that. Of course, faith feels complicated because everything else is complicated. Life is a treasure of riches, and guttural pain. One day you're texting your dad a photo of your newly planted flower beds and the next he has passed out in the shower and the scan of his brain is gray with cancerous growth. Life is both things at the same time, the quick flight home for the surgery and the tearful snuggle in his hospital bed.

"Barn's burnt down," Mizuta Masahide wrote, "now I can see the moon."[1] I think of this as I sit beside Jonah, watching him color his card for Ace in Leah's kitchen eight years after our babies were born and our church broke open. I think of how our friendship is deeper than it ever would have been had we not hurt each other, forgiven each other, learned to embrace and hold tight to each other as our babies came into the world. It feels like a miracle that even now, living on opposite sides of the country, I get to bake her son's birthday cake on a Thursday afternoon in April during a particularly painful week for her family. This is beauty built on what once looked like wreckage.

· · ·

"Jesus shows us how to understand who God is," I say to that room of teenagers two days later.

This poem Jesus recites, this list of *makarioi*—with its upside-down logic and wild ideas that we who suffer are the whole ones, that we in our limits, in our weaknesses, are the ones who find the spiritual life that brings us to flourishing—I can't help but believe it. In the quiet suffering following a loved one's death, in the uncertain anxiety of daily life, and even in the social and economic inequalities found in our society's unspoken but always-evil caste system, Jesus's poem offers a way to live within the realness of the pain, and also in the hope of something truer, better—the dream of God.

Catholic oblate and beloved author Ronald Rolheiser says, "Desire can show itself as aching pain or delicious hope. Spirituality is, ultimately, about what we do with that desire."[2]

On the last morning of the retreat, I show the students an image drawn by artist and modern iconographer Scott Erickson. It's a lighthouse that stands on ground that has been formed on the wreckage of a ship. It's obvious that time has covered the ship's wreckage with land, creating the island on which the lighthouse stands. The image is called *Lighthouse Shipwreck*. The description that accompanies it reads, "Your greatest shipwreck becomes the way in which you give the brightest light to the world."[3]

Throughout the weekend, I've read aloud the passage from Matthew 5 to the students, Jesus's poem of *makarioi*. And now we've come to the next paragraph: "You are the light of the world," Jesus says to the people, the same ones he just blessed in their grief, in their suffering, in their meekness and mercy. "You, already, are the light of the world."

I say this to my audience of teenagers. Some still in masks. One or two sneaking looks at the phones in their laps. Some gay, some straight, some hiding family secrets, some holding unspoken exhaustion, grief, or endless insecurity. You are the light of the world.

"He doesn't say, 'Do these things and you'll be the light of the world.' He doesn't give them the Beatitudes and insist that if they climb some impossible ladder they'll finally be good enough to let their light shine." I look at the teenagers sitting before me, some I have known since they were third graders in my 2013 Sunday school class, and some I have only just met. "You are already the light of the world. Your light rises up, not in spite of the shipwrecks of your life but right there, in the middle of them. Maybe even because of them."

I think about who I was before the prenatal diagnosis that changed everything, who I was staring into the mirror in my glitter lioness shirt, inviting God to bring my child—exactly as he was—into the world through me. *I receive him.* I think about my body on my knees in the hallway outside August's room begging for breath, knowing that my failures as a parent might mark him forever.

"This is what grace is," I say. "It is never that the shipwreck doesn't come. It's that the land grows out of it. And that is where your light shines brightest."

● ● ●

Several days before, on Ace's birthday, we all gathered around the table after finishing the birthday song while August, fourteen, and Brooks, newly twelve, tried again to teach Ace to blow out his candles. All of us circling the table, centering his little face, his wide eyes entranced by the eight candles flickering on his gluten-free cake.

"Ace, like this, buddy," August said, mimicking the song we'd been practicing for this very moment. "The train goes choo choo," my teenager, now six foot three, said, while he pursed his lips and blew, his long, blond surfer hair grazing the tops of his shoulders. Ace kneeled on the chair next to his dad, as his brothers leaned their large-boy bodies across the table toward him, close enough to demonstrate the task they'd been trying to teach Ace since his first birthday seven years ago.

"Actually," Brooks said, "blowing out candles is pretty unsanitary when you think about it." August turned his head to scowl at his brother, annoyed. "It's true!" Brooks said.

Ace looked from the flames to his brothers' faces, smiling. He brought his lips together, and no air emerged. Brooks tried again. "Like Thomas, Ace. Choo! Choo!" Ace smiled wide and pushed out an open-mouthed breath.

"Hey, pretty close!" I said, hovering near enough to Ace's chair to catch his hand if he reached out to touch the flames. Ace turned his face to me and grinned. "Aahdahdah!"

"Okay! Everybody! All together!" Chris said. And we all blew, Ace giggling, flapping his hands.

Eight candles lit up our small dining room, then gave way to our shared breath, transforming flame into white smoke, all curls and magic. I imagined my light lifting from this table and rising into the world, shimmering into the sky.

Maybe this is what wholeness looks like, I thought, our whoops rising up to meet the smoke. *Makarioi*, here in the dream of God. Light shining true, all the way through.

ACKNOWLEDGMENTS

So much thanks to my writing partners, Cara Meredith and Erin Lane, who walked me through every stage of this book, from concussion recovery and COVID-19 lockdown to the brilliant idea that this wasn't just a book about Ace; it was a book about the Beatitudes. Thank you both for the endless conversations, laughter, and always faithful feedback.

Also thanks to Lauren Winner and the Collegeville Institute. Lauren spent time with early chapters, and my conversations with her clarified the trajectory of this book. And my time at the Collegeville Institute offered ten glorious days in Minnesota to walk in the woods, swim in the lake, write this book, and grieve my dad's death.

I'm grateful to Catherine Ricketts and Amy Julia Becker, who both provided last-minute and necessary feedback during the final weeks of my manuscript writing. As did Mercedes Lara and Heather Avis, my dear partners on *The Lucky Few* podcast. Also, many thanks to Kelli Caughman, who offered her particular expertise on the intersection of race and Down syndrome. And I'm grateful to my brother and lifelong writing mentor, Jason Boyett, for the help with design and always-quick opinions.

Writing chapter 7 was a doozy. I'm grateful to Jonathan Merritt for giving his eye and experience to an early version. And also to my fellow elders of 2015, who helped me remember timeline details, and my friend and former pastor Fred Harrell, who read an early draft and provided wisdom in how to think about the loss of that season. I'm most grateful for my friends Leah and Jared, who continue to so remarkably live in the service of peace that they not only gave me permission to write about our friendship and about their son but also demanded I change the chapter when I was too hard on myself when telling our story of loss and healing. I love you both. Also, Jonah? You're the coolest. Thanks for letting me write about you too, buddy.

Thanks to my pastor, Michael Rudzena, for his faithful help with theological sources and for his weekly sermons, where his rigorous study and reimagination of the teaching of Jesus has shaped how I approach scripture. I wouldn't have discovered "the dream of God" without his first pointing me to Stephanie Spellers. Thank you to my friend Jeff Chu for not only helping with chapter 7 but also pointing out that giant, glaring mistake with the Greek! (Also, Jeff, that flower bouquet really did show up just when I needed it most.)

This book was written in San Francisco and Morristown and researched in New York City. But it owes much of its shape and tone to the guest room at Stone Bridge Farm in Newton, New Jersey, where Jerusalem, Nathan, and Wylie Greer opened their home to me over and over while I snuck away from my family and focused on my sentences. Thank you all for living out your value to hospitality by making space for me.

I'm grateful to my agent, Zoë Pagnamenta, for her support and belief in me and this project. Also, Katelyn Beaty, thanks for making this book the most beautiful version of itself. I'm grateful for the rest of the team at Brazos, especially Paula Gibson,

Erin Smith, Melinda Timmer, and Julie Zahm, along with all the unseen hands that worked on this manuscript.

To the Good Shepherd youth group, thank you for being such an important part of my spiritual community and for cheering this book on.

To my kids: Aug, it takes a lot of courage to share parts of our story that aren't our shiniest. Thanks for trusting me with yours. Don't ever forget that our lights glow, not despite of our weaknesses but right there in the middle of them. You are hilarious, compassionate, and a great friend. I'm so proud of you and your giant teenage self.

Brooksie, the *you* in these pages could never match the shimmering, interesting human I get to know in real life. I love your thoughtful, inquisitive nature, and how, even now as an almost-teenager, you're still pointing to the mercy in the people around you. Also, I'm glad your room was next to my office when I worked on this book. Your rendition of "Smells Like Teen Spirit" is my favorite writing music, always and forever.

And Ace, I know that at this moment in your life you couldn't give me permission to write about you, so I pray you're honored in these pages. Someday, I hope you'll read this and know how much you were loved at this stage of your life. You changed everything for me, and I'm endlessly grateful for what you've taught me about wholeness and flourishing and Jesus.

Christopher, my co-rememberer: this book wouldn't exist if you hadn't made sacrifices so I could hole up and churn it out. Thanks for bearing with me and encouraging me to keep trying to say the things that matter most. I didn't even mention your superman jaw this time. Aren't you proud?

I lost my dad at the beginning stages of writing this manuscript. Pops and I differed on a lot of things theologically, but when it came to Ace, his youngest grandbaby, we both carried the same tender love. I was honored to be beside him—and with my dear siblings and Mom—when he, with courage and great faith, moved "further up and further in," and I felt the gift of his life deeply as I wrote these pages. You don't have to agree on theology to agree on the remarkable person of Jesus. And I'm grateful for the countless ways my dad taught me to love and explore scripture, to seek a life of wisdom, and to be mesmerized by a good story. I'm so grateful to have had a dad who loved me and loved a good idea.

NOTES

Prologue The Dream of God

1. This translation of Matthew 5:1–2 is from Jonathan T. Pennington, *The Sermon on the Mount and Human Flourishing*, 2nd ed. (Grand Rapids: Baker Academic, 2018), xv.

2. Some examples of Jesus healing those who would have been considered "unclean" by touching them can be found in Matthew 8:1–4 and 9:23–26.

3. By "postscript," I mean the resurrection, a culmination of the story of Jesus that lights up all that came before it.

4. The exact site of the Sermon on the Mount is unknown, but it's traditionally assumed that Jesus taught his listeners along the northwestern shore of the Sea of Galilee on a hill now known as the Mount of the Beatitudes or Mount Eremos, which is part of the Korazim Plateau. See https://www.seetheholyland.net/tag/mount-eremos or https://www.touristisrael.com/mount-of-beatitudes/28175.

5. The Greco-Roman virtue tradition was asking, "What is happiness, blessedness, *šālôm*, and how does one obtain and sustain it?" Pennington, *Sermon on the Mount*, 14.

6. *Beatitudes* is derived from the Latin *beatus*, meaning "happy, fortunate, blissful." Jim Forest, *The Ladder of the Beatitudes* (Maryknoll, NY: Orbis Books, 1999), 17.

7. Flourishing is a fairly new way of translating *macarioi*. Pennington has received some pushback on his argument that "flourish" is an accurate translation.

8. Walter Brueggemann discusses the idea of an "alternative script" in his lecture "A Script to Live (and to Die) By: 19 Theses," given at the Emergent Theological Conversation, September 13–15, 2004, All Souls Fellowship, Decatur, GA.

9. Scot McKnight, *Sermon on the Mount*, The Story of God Bible Commentary (Grand Rapids: Zondervan, 2013), 31. This was also helpfully found via Pennington's scholarship.

10. Servais Pinckaers, OP, *The Pursuit of Happiness—God's Way: Living the Beatitudes*, trans. Mary Thomas Noble, OP, 2nd ed. (Eugene, OR: Wipf & Stock, 2008), viii. Jonathan Pennington also pointed me to this source.

11. It covers Matthew 5–7.

12. A sermon on the Beatitudes given by my pastor, Michael Rudzena, helped me find these words. He asked the question, How is God showing up in the world and how would we know if we were to come across it? "Good Shepherd New York, 1.29.23," service on January 29, 2023, YouTube video, 1:21:46, https://www.youtube.com/watch?v=248LK3gWL9k.

13. Brueggemann, "Script to Live (and to Die) By."

14. "A macarism is a *makarios* statement that ascribes happiness or flourishing to a particular person or state. A macarism is a pronouncement, based on observation, that a certain way of being in the world produces human flourishing and felicity. Macarisms were widespread throughout the ancient world, within Judaism and without. The Sermon begins with a strong series of macarisms." Pennington, *Sermon on the Mount*, 42.

15. Samson L. Uytanlet, with Kiem-Kiok Kwa, *Matthew: A Pastoral and Contextual Commentary*, Asia Bible Commentary Series (Carlisle, UK: Langham Global Library, 2017), 51–52.

16. Stephanie Spellers, *The Church Cracked Open: Disruption, Decline, and New Hope for Beloved Community* (New York: Church Publishing, 2021), 7.

17. Richard Rohr, *Jesus' Plan for a New World: The Sermon on the Mount* (Cincinnati: Franciscan Media, 1996), 29.

Chapter 1 For the Weak Ones

1. See Matthew 14:14 and 15:32.

2. Frederick Dale Bruner, *Matthew: A Commentary*, vol. 1, *The Christbook: Matthew 1–12* (Grand Rapids: Eerdmans, 2004), 158.

3. Dallas Willard, *The Divine Conspiracy: Rediscovering Our Hidden Life in God* (New York: HarperSanFrancisco, 1994), 108.

4. Richard Rohr, *Jesus' Plan for a New World: The Sermon on the Mount* (Cincinnati: Franciscan Media, 1996), 63.

5. Bruner, *Matthew*, 160.

6. Bruner, *Matthew*, 158–59.

7. Bruner, *Matthew*, 158–59.

8. Bruner, *Matthew*, 160.

9. My favorite scene in C. S. Lewis's *The Last Battle* describes the new world that awaits his characters: "Come further up, come further in!" (New York: HarperCollins, 1984), 209. Here in this life, I imagine our souls inviting us to move inward toward a deeper knowing: further down, further out, deeper and broader than we knew we could go.

10. Throughout his commentary on the Sermon on the Mount, Scot McKnight refers to "the good life," an idea similar to Pennington's "human flourishing." *Sermon on the Mount*, The Story of God Bible Commentary (Grand Rapids: Zondervan, 2013), 32.

11. Barbara Brown Taylor, *An Altar in the World: A Geography of Faith* (New York: HarperOne, 2009), 206.

12. Richard Lischer, "The Sermon on the Mount as Radical Pastoral Care," *Interpretation: A Journal of Bible and Theology* 41, no. 2 (1987): 164.

13. W. D. Davies, *Matthew: A Shorter Commentary*, ed. Dale C. Allison (New York: T&T Clark, 2001), 65.

14. Stanley Hauerwas describes this vision of community as "a diversity that creates not envy but cooperation and love." "Living the Proclaimed Reign of God: A Sermon on the Sermon on the Mount," *Interpretation: A Journal of Bible and Theology* 47, no. 2 (1987): 157.

15. Bruner, *Matthew*, 160.

16. Bruner, *Matthew*, 160.

Chapter 2 For the Ones Who Grieve

1. "Whether in Ancient Rome, Ancient Greece, the pre-Columbian Americas, Medieval Japan or Medieval England, the European Renaissance, or Imperial China: Every fourth newborn died in the first year of life. One out of two died in childhood." Anthony A. Volk and Jeremy A. Atkinson, "Infant and Child Death in the Human Environment of Evolutionary Adaptation," *Evolution and Human Behavior* 34, no. 3 (2013): 182–92. An abstract of this article is available at https://www.sciencedirect.com/science/article/pii/S1090513812001237#s0015.

2. Jonathan T. Pennington, *The Sermon on the Mount and Human Flourishing*, 2nd ed. (Grand Rapids: Baker Academic, 2018), 149.

3. Jim Forest, *The Ladder of the Beatitudes* (Maryknoll, NY: Orbis Books, 1999), 38.

4. Servais Pinckaers, OP, *The Pursuit of Happiness—God's Way: Living the Beatitudes*, trans. Mary Thomas Noble, OP, 2nd ed. (Eugene, OR: Wipf & Stock, 2008), 36–37.

5. Forest, *Ladder of the Beatitudes*, 46.

6. See Psalm 126:6 (NRSVue).

Chapter 3 For the Ones Who Release Their Power

1. For one example of academic research concerning the value of placing students with Down syndrome in inclusive educational settings, see J. Hughes, "Inclusive Education for Individuals with Down Syndrome," *Down Syndrome News and Update* 6, no. 1 (2006): 1–3, doi:10.3104/practice.370. See also S. Buckley, G. Bird, B. Sacks, and T. Archer, "A Comparison of Mainstream and Special Education for Teenagers with Down Syndrome: Implications for Parents and Teachers," *Down Syndrome News and Update* 2, no. 2 (2002): 46–54.

2. See Heather Avis and Sarah Mensinga, *Everyone Belongs* (Colorado Springs: Waterbrook, 2022). This is my favorite book to use for helping children think about disability and inclusive practices.

3. Scot McKnight describes the blessings of the Beatitudes as "the entire history of the philosophy of the 'good life' and the late modern theory of 'happiness' ... at work." *Sermon on the Mount*, The Story of God Bible Commentary (Grand Rapids: Zondervan, 2013), 32.

4. The origin of the phrase "personal salvation project" is commonly attributed to Thomas Merton.

5. Ranier Marie Rilke, "Let This Darkness Be a Bell Tower," in *In Praise of Mortality: Selections from Rainer Maria Rilke's Duino Elegies and Sonnets to Orpheus*, trans. Joanna Macy and Anita Barrows (Brattleboro, VT: Echo Point Books & Media, 2016), 29.

6. The use of the word "flourishing" as a translation of "makarioi" is from Jonathan T. Pennington, *The Sermon on the Mount and Human Flourishing*, 2nd

ed. (Grand Rapids: Baker Academic, 2018), xv. The phrase "inherit the world" is also borrowed from Pennington.

7. Rilke, "Let This Darkness Be a Bell Tower," 135.

8. Samson L. Uytanlet, with Kiem-Kiok Kwa, *Matthew: A Pastoral and Contextual Commentary*, Asia Bible Commentary Series (Carlisle, UK: Langham Global Library, 2017), 53.

9. Jim Forest, *The Ladder of the Beatitudes* (Maryknoll, NY: Orbis Books, 1999), 48.

10. Richard Rohr, with John Bookser Feister, "Blessed Are the Gentle," Center for Action and Contemplation, January 31, 2018, https://cac.org/daily-meditations/blessed-are-the-gentle-2018-01-31/. The wording for Psalm 37:11 in the text is the wording used in this article.

11. Rohr, with Feister, "Blessed Are the Gentle." This article is short but incredibly helpful for anyone looking to deepen their understanding of this particular passage.

12. Rohr, with Feister, "Blessed Are the Gentle."

13. "Beloved community" was originally an idea pioneered by Josiah Royce, a white idealist philosopher in the late nineteenth century. Howard Thurman, Martin Luther King Jr, and Dietrich Bonhoeffer propelled his ideas forward, particularly in how they applied it to Jesus's vision of the kingdom of God.

14. Stephanie Spellers, *The Church Cracked Open: Disruption, Decline, and New Hope for Beloved Community* (New York: Church Publishing, 2021), 25.

15. Spellers, *Church Cracked Open*, 26.

16. Howard Thurman, *Jesus and the Disinherited*, 3rd ed. (Boston: Beacon, 1996), 38.

17. Mark Scandrette, *The Ninefold Path of Jesus: Hidden Wisdom of the Beatitudes* (Downers Grove, IL: InterVarsity, 2018), 55.

Chapter 4 For the Ones Who Long for Justice

1. Jonathan T. Pennington, *The Sermon on the Mount and Human Flourishing*, 2nd ed. (Grand Rapids: Baker Academic, 2018), 42–67.

2. Frederick Dale Bruner writes, "When Matthew's Jesus then explicates this wretchedness as being also 'poor in spirit,' he wishes to say that [for] those who have reached the bottom spiritually, emotionally, and psychically . . . *God is especially there.*" *Matthew: A Commentary*, vol. 1, *The Christbook: Matthew 1–12* (Grand Rapids: Eerdmans, 2004), 160, emphasis added.

3. Jim Forest, *The Ladder of the Beatitudes* (Maryknoll, NY: Orbis Books, 1999), 62.

4. Gregory Boyle, *Tattoos on the Heart: The Power of Boundless Compassion*, 2nd ed. (New York: Free Press, 2011), 75.

5. Andy Crouch, *The Life We're Looking For: Reclaiming Relationship in a Technological World* (New York: Convergent, 2022), 75.

6. Crouch, *The Life We're Looking For*, 76.

7. Isabel Wilkerson, *Caste: The Origins of Our Discontent*, 4th ed. (New York: Random House, 2020), 48.

8. Stephanie Spellers, *The Church Cracked Open: Disruption, Decline, and New Hope for Beloved Community* (New York: Church Publishing, 2021), 28.

9. Crouch, *The Life We're Looking For*, 76.

10. Spellers, *Church Cracked Open*, 26.

11. Howard Thurman says that "love is possible only between two freed spirits." *Jesus and the Disinherited*, 3rd ed. (Boston: Beacon, 1996), 9.

Chapter 5 For the Ones Who Give Mercy

1. Kelley Nikondeha, *The First Advent in Palestine: Reversals, Resistance, and the Ongoing Complexity of Hope* (Minneapolis: Broadleaf Books, 2022). Kelley's book uses the word *reversal* in a beautiful and compelling way.

2. See Stanley Hauerwas, "Living the Proclaimed Reign of God: A Sermon on the Sermon on the Mount," *Interpretation: A Journal of Bible and Theology* 47, no. 2 (1987): 117–26.

3. Mark Scandrette, *The Ninefold Path of Jesus: Hidden Wisdom of the Beatitudes* (Downers Grove, IL: InterVarsity, 2018), 75.

4. Jim Forest, *The Ladder of the Beatitudes* (Maryknoll, NY: Orbis Books, 1999), 78.

5. Forest, *Ladder of the Beatitudes*, 80.

6. See Psalm 51:1: "Have mercy upon me, O God, according to Your lovingkindness" (NKJV). I owe this insight to Forest, *Ladder of the Beatitudes*, 80.

7. Psalm 25:10 (NKJV).

8. Matthew 5:43–44 (NIV).

9. Scandrette, *Ninefold Path of Jesus*, 72.

10. Frederick Dale Bruner, *Matthew: A Commentary*, vol. 1, *The Christbook: Matthew 1–12* (Grand Rapids: Eerdmans, 2004), 173.

11. Saint Isaac of Syria, "Directions in Spiritual Training," quoted in Forest, *Ladder of the Beatitudes*, 89.

Chapter 6 For the True Ones

1. Jim Forest, *The Ladder of the Beatitudes* (Maryknoll, NY: Orbis Books, 1999), 92–93.

2. Frederick Dale Bruner, *Matthew: A Commentary*, vol. 1, *The Christbook: Matthew 1–12* (Grand Rapids: Eerdmans, 2004), 175.

3. Bruner, *Matthew*, 175.

4. Mark Scandrette, *The Ninefold Path of Jesus: Hidden Wisdom of the Beatitudes* (Downers Grove, IL: InterVarsity, 2018), 86.

5. Thomas Merton, *New Seeds of Contemplation*, 3rd ed. (New York: New Directions, 2007), 20.

6. Merton, *New Seeds of Contemplation*, 295.

7. Richard Rohr, *Falling Upward: A Spirituality for the Two Halves of Life* (San Francisco: Jossey-Bass, 2011), 85–86.

8. Parker J. Palmer, *Let Your Life Speak: Listening for the Voice of Vocation* (San Francisco: Jossey-Bass, 2000), 85.

9. Scandrette, *Ninefold Path of Jesus*, 127.

10. John 14:17 (NRSVA).

Chapter 7 For the Ones Who Serve Peace

1. These statistics come from Jeremy J. Gibbs, "Religious Conflict, Sexual Identity, and Suicidal Behaviors among LGBT Young Adults," *Archives of Suicide Research* 19, no. 4 (2015): 472–88, https://www.ncbi.nlm.nih.gov/pmc/articles/PMC4706071/.

2. See Galatians 5:22–23.

3. Jim Forest, *The Ladder of the Beatitudes* (Maryknoll, NY: Orbis Books, 1999), 112.

4. Lynch, quoted in Forest, *Ladder of the Beatitudes*, 122.

5. I have since come to a place where I don't believe in membership in churches, which is a story for another time. Writing about my own vote to determine whether people could be "in" or "out" within the church causes me no small amount of discomfort. I don't believe the notion of membership is representative of the way of Jesus.

6. This story is found in Acts 8:26–40. The Ethiopian eunuch is often seen as the first gentile convert to Christianity. He was also the first African convert. By some scholars, he has been considered to be a representative of the queer community, as often eunuchs were objects of sexual desire to both males and females.

7. By "nonessential," I'm referring to any idea that isn't creedal to Christianity—that is, about the life, death, and resurrection of Jesus. Ken Wilson, in his book *A Letter to My Congregation* (Canton, MI: Front Edge, 2014), spells out this notion of a third way, using the example of Romans 11, a passage in which Paul speaks to a church controversy involving food sacrificed to idols. Some members of the Roman church held the conviction that food sacrificed to idols could not be eaten because it was tainted by idol worship, while others held the conviction that it was just food and that idol worship had no power over it. Wilson acknowledges that there is room for both viewpoints to exist and for the church to continue to worship together.

8. Stanley Hauerwas, "Living the Proclaimed Reign of God: A Sermon on the Sermon on the Mount," *Interpretation: A Journal of Bible and Theology* 47, no. 2 (1987): 157.

9. Hauerwas, "Living the Proclaimed Reign of God," 157–58.

10. My pastor's interpretation of this instruction from Jesus, found later in the Sermon on the Mount, was transformative for my understanding of what Jesus means when he says "Turn the other cheek." In this interpretation, Jesus is commanding us not to invite more abuse but to respond with nonviolent courage with the part of us that has not yet been abused: the other cheek. Michael Rudzena, "Good Shepherd New York, 2.5.23," service on February 5, 2023, YouTube video, 57:09, https://www.youtube.com/watch?v=Ylwqg2ful5g.

11. Ronald Rolheiser, *The Holy Longing: The Search for a Christian Spirituality* (New York: Image Books, 1999), 180.

12. See Rolheiser, *Holy Longing*. Rolheiser quotes extensively from a series of talks Jim Wallace gave in 1986 titled "On Peacemaking," which explains, "All of our actions for peace must be rooted in the power of love and the power of truth. . . . Our motivation must always be to open people to the truth and not to show ourselves as right and them as wrong" (181). Wallace's series of talks can be obtained on audiobook through Sojourners: Sojourners, 2401 13th Street NW, Washington, DC 20009.

13. Dani Blum, "The Joy in Finding Your Chosen Family," *New York Times*, June 25, 2022, https://www.nytimes.com/2022/06/25/well/lgbtq-chosen-families.html.

14. This wording is taken from the New Revised Standard Version, updated edition (NRSVue).

15. Sandra Marie Schneiders, "The Lamb of God and the Forgiveness of Sin(s) in the Fourth Gospel," *Catholic Biblical Quarterly* 73, no. 1 (2011): 1–29. In most of our English translations, John 20:23 says, "If you forgive the sins of any, they are

forgiven them; if you retain the sins of any, they are retained" (NRSVue). This has been taken by many to mean that Jesus gave his apostles special ability to give or refuse God's forgiveness through the Holy Spirit. Schneiders's interpretation aligns more fully with previous teachings of Jesus as well as cultural and language dynamics at play.

16. My pastor, Michael Rudzena, opened up this passage beautifully in his sermon on John 20. "Good Shepherd New York, 5.28.23," service on May 28, 2023, YouTube video, 1:04:10, https://www.youtube.com/watch?v=3ZxlFtvorNg.

17. I don't have space here to include the story of Florence, another dear friend who suffered immensely during this crisis in our church, who showed up, four-month-old baby in hand, to make me soup, clean my toilets, and fold my family's clothes while I was on bed rest, all when she had plenty of right to be angry with my leadership decisions. Her kindness and courage have been transformative in my life.

18. Rolheiser, *Holy Longing*, 184.

19. Rolheiser, *Holy Longing*, 188.

Chapter 8 For the Ones Who Suffer for Doing Good

1. Jonathan T. Pennington, *The Sermon on the Mount and Human Flourishing*, 2nd ed. (Grand Rapids: Baker Academic, 2018), 148–49.

2. Justin Hawkins has a beautiful article, "Dignity beyond Accomplishment," Mere Orthodoxy, January 19, 2021, https://mereorthodoxy.com/dignity-beyond-accomplishment/. He was interviewed about his article on my podcast, *The Lucky Few*, June 1, 2021, https://podcasts.apple.com/lu/podcast/117-discussing-dignity-beyond-accomplishment-article/id1349646917?i=1000523750847.

3. *Ted Lasso*, season 2, episode 7, "Headspace," directed by Matt Lipsey, written by Phoebe Walsh, aired September 3, 2021, on Apple TV+.

4. What a simple but profound idea. It comes from Mark Scandrette, *The Ninefold Path of Jesus: Hidden Wisdom of the Beatitudes* (Downers Grove, IL: InterVarsity, 2018), 119–20.

5. Scandrette, *Ninefold Path of Jesus*, 119–20.

6. This phrase, of course, comes from the great civil rights leader and congressman John Lewis.

Chapter 9 For the Fearless Ones

1. I'm grateful to Isabel Wilkerson for all her ideas around caste as it relates to race in America in her book *Caste: The Origins of Our Discontent*, 4th ed. (New York: Random House, 2020).

2. Matthew 5:11–12 (NASB).

3. Gregory Boyle, *Tattoos on the Heart: The Power of Boundless Compassion*, 2nd ed. (New York: Free Press, 2011), 75.

4. Mark Scandrette, *The Ninefold Path of Jesus: Hidden Wisdom of the Beatitudes* (Downers Grove, IL: InterVarsity, 2018), 129.

5. Scandrette, *Ninefold Path of Jesus*, 129.

6. Scandrette, *Ninefold Path of Jesus*, 129.

7. I highly recommend Scandrette's book *The Ninefold Path of Jesus*, which takes readers through each of these "postures" of the Beatitudes as a way of spiritual practice.

8. See Revelation 21:5.

9. Jonathan T. Pennington, *The Sermon on the Mount and Human Flourishing*, 2nd ed. (Grand Rapids: Baker Academic, 2018), 147.

10. Patricia Farris, "Be Happy!," *Christian Century*, January 26, 2005, https://www.religion-online.org/article/be-happy-micah-61-8-matthew-51-12/.

11. Scandrette, *Ninefold Path of Jesus*, 127.

12. Anna Case-Winters, *Matthew:* Belief: A Theological Commentary on the Bible (Louisville: Westminster John Knox, 2015), 78.

13. Frederick Dale Bruner, *Matthew: A Commentary*, vol. 1, *The Christbook: Matthew 1–12* (Grand Rapids: Eerdmans, 2004), 182.

14. Pennington, *Sermon on the Mount*, 150.

15. Pennington, *Sermon on the Mount*, 159.

16. Bruner, *Matthew*, 182.

17. I appreciated this simplification from Farris, "Be Happy!"

18. This quote is from the Work of the People, "Transforming through Love: Part 1," https://www.theworkofthepeople.com/transforming-through-love-part-one.

Epilogue For the Lights of the World

1. Mizuta Masahide was a seventeenth-century Japanese poet, and this haiku was his most renowned bit of poetry.

2. Ronald Rolheiser, *The Holy Longing: The Search for a Christian Spirituality* (New York: Image Books, 1999), 5.

3. The image can be viewed at https://scotterricksonartshop.com/products/lighthouse-shipwreck.